THE
DREAM

Keith Miller

THE DREAM

WORD BOOKS
PUBLISHER
WACO, TEXAS

A DIVISION OF
WORD, INCORPORATED

THE DREAM

Library of Congress Cataloging in Publication Data:

Miller, Keith.
    The dream.

    1. Christianity — 20th century.   2. Church.   I. Title.
BR121.2.M485   1985   262'.0017   84-27018
ISBN 0–8499–0462–5

Printed in the United States of America

FOR ANDREA
who continues to amaze me with her love and courage,
and whose example keeps drawing me on
to want to risk living
God's dream.

Introduction

The following pages were dictated during an eight-hour period beginning at about 10:00 P.M. on 1 May 1984. My wife was in Oklahoma, and I was alone in the house. I had not been preparing to write a manuscript and had never even thought about doing a book like this one. I was dictating some correspondence into a dictation machine when my train of thought was interrupted. For six hours I dictated the new thoughts which came flooding into my mind. Then I fell asleep, woke up, and dictated for two more hours. During that time the material on the following pages came to me in substantially the same form in which you find it here.

This was a unique and very moving creative experience for me, and it is exciting—if a little frightening—to share it with you. I am not claiming that this is an actual auditory conversation and journey with God. I used the dramatic form of an evening spent with the Presence because that is the way the content presented itself to me that night in May.

KEITH MILLER
Port Aransas, Texas

THE DREAM

1

The darkness was pitch black. I was up on my elbows in bed, alone because my wife, Andrea, was out of town. The wind was still howling from a storm which had come in from the Gulf of Mexico the evening before.

Suddenly I heard a voice, a voice deeper than Tennessee Ernie Ford's. It resounded from the upper right-hand corner of the room in the darkness, and it spoke my name: "Keith."

I couldn't say anything. I was paralyzed with fear. I had no idea to whom the voice belonged. And then it spoke again: "KEITH, I'm talking to you; can you hear me?"

All of a sudden I realized Who it was that was paying me a visit. Now I was really afraid. There was no way this could be happening. My heart was pounding so loudly I could hardly hear the words. I answered in a voice that was husky with sleep . . . and fear. "Yes, Sir, ah . . ."

My eyes were straining in the dark toward the part of the room from which the voice was coming. I could see only a kind of blur, like a gray shadow moving and shifting, lighter than the rest of the blackness. Or was it my imagination?

Before I had time to think, I could hear it speaking again, "Keith, are you ready to follow Me?"

"Yes, sir, I . . . am." I said without moving in the bed.

"I mean *Right now!*" the Presence demanded.

Terror. Then I heard a very small childlike voice come out of me. "Where are we going?" I asked.

There was a pause. Then, "Keith, my heart is about to break. I've been frustrated for years about what's going on in My church, and lately I've been getting very angry! I want to take you with Me and show you what's happening."

"Why?" I asked, still frightened.

"Because I want you to tell My people what you will see," He answered.

I shrank back. "Oh no, you've got the wrong person. I've had lots of problems—still do—and the church is not looking for a direct message from You through me."

"But I've *chosen* you to tell them," He said, sounding a little impatient.

"Why me?" I persisted. (I didn't want any part of this assignment.)

"Well," the Presence answered slowly, "because the other people I thought of are all engaged in important ministries for Me. And since you're not exactly exhausting yourself loving other people, you're the one."

I lay there for about thirty seconds, thinking about what He'd said. Then suddenly the house was filled with the loudest voice I'd ever heard—almost a roar.

"GET UP!" His voice shook the room.

I threw my feet out of the bed and sat there blinking, not knowing quite what to do. Then I felt something like a huge, powerful hand—only twice as soft—simply lift me as if I were a feather. As my eyes got accustomed to the light I could see that I was being carried like a small child in the arms of a Person.

We went out through the closed window—without breaking it, in fact, without *touching* it—and into the night. The storm had subsided; the air was quiet and clean, and I could smell the rain-soaked earth. We sailed up, up, up, brushing a palm frond on a fifty-foot tree as we flew by.

Before long we were high above the coastline, and the moon turned the tops of the clouds into a rolling, snow-white fairyland rimmed in silvery light. We moved in absolute silence. I clung to the Presence like a baby monkey clings to its mother, although I felt a little foolish since there wasn't really anything tangible to hold onto. Gradually, however, my panic subsided, because I felt a strange security in the arms of the Presence.

I asked again, hesitantly, "Where are we going?" There was silence for some minutes. And I was afraid to ask anything more.

And then the voice from the Presence said, "I'm glad you decided to come."

"*Decided?*" I blurted out, but then thought better of what I had started to say. I commented instead, "I see why you've chosen me—I've got to be one of the biggest sinners around. Listen, I'm really sorry for all of the bad things I've done . . . and for the things I haven't done that I should have . . ."

"No," He said. "I'm not mad at you for those things. You've already repented and confessed them, and I've forgiven you as I said I would. But there are some things I've been seeing in My church recently that are hurting Me and making Me very *angry!* And those are the things I want you to tell people about."

"Uh, would it be poss . . ." I began in a low voice, which finally died out.

"What are you mumbling about?" He said.

"I . . . I'd just as soon not do this if You don't mind, Sir," I said in a small voice.

"Keith, why are you afraid to tell them what I want you to?"

"Well," I said, "If You're as upset about things as You seem to be, I don't think people hearing about it are going to be too happy with the one who tells them."

"Look," He said, "I'm only going to show you the truth. How can they be so upset about the truth? After all they're My people! They're Christians."

"Well," I said hesitantly, "With all due respect, Sir, Your record hasn't been too good with those You've sent to tell Your people . . ."

"Well," He said, "I still want to keep trying to reach them. And nowadays we've got a lot more committed people in the church; maybe they'll pay attention to what you tell them in My name."

I mumbled, "I sure hope You're right."

"What are you saying?" He said.

"Well, Sir, I've had a lot of rejection from some of Your people. And . . . well . . . it just doesn't seem to make very good sense for *me* to be the one to tell them the truth about what *You* see."

"Listen, Miller, why do you think I've taken you through all the pain and agony of the last few years? I let your writings become well known, and I gave you all of the attention and material things you could use. Then, when you came crashing down—largely because of your own sin and stupidity—you wound up with an aching heart, a fragmented ministry, and a badly bruised ego. But I had to let you get there so you could hear Me and depend on Me and understand firsthand about My love and grace and forgiveness."

"Yes," I said doubtfully, "I guess I really did need to go through all that—if You say so. And I certainly do appreciate Your hanging around."

"Well, it isn't that you're such great shakes now," He said. "You're still pretty focused on your own agenda. I don't want to rub it in, but I had to wait until ten o'clock at night before I could even get your attention!"

2

I was about to answer something to defend myself when suddenly I felt my stomach rush up into my throat. We must have dropped four hundred feet. The Presence said, "Oh, sorry about that, but this is our first stop."

We disappeared into the clouds for what seemed like twenty seconds before we dropped through the pillowy cloud-quilt and back into the light from the high white moon. Far below us I could see the blinking lights of a city that we were approaching at dive-bomber speed. I held on to the Presence for dear life.

As we got closer I saw we were heading right for a large, dark church steeple. There were some lights on in a wing off to the side of the building. As we circled past the front of the church I tried to make out the name, but all I could see was "First . . . (something) Church." By this time we were hovering outside the window of a room in which a meeting was taking place.

The Presence whispered to me, "Just keep quiet and listen. I want you to hear this."

I whispered back, "We're not going *in* there, are . . . ?"

Before I had time to finish, we were in the room, standing in the corner. I felt stupid in my pajamas and wanted to hide somewhere. But then I realized that someone was looking right at me and didn't see me, so I relaxed and looked around. A big, red-faced man in an expensive business suit was standing up and almost shouting at someone across the room.

"I don't care if he has done a good job for ten years, the secretary claimed he tried to talk her into having sex with him!"

I turned to the Presence. "Wow!" I said.

"Shh! Listen."

A meek-looking man sitting across the room was obviously agitated too. He said, as strongly as he could, "But he *denies* it!"

"Listen," the big man said, as if reasoning with a small child. "We just announced a three-million-dollar building fund campaign last weekend. If it gets out that we're tolerating sin among the staff, our new building won't have an ice cube's chance in hell—if you'll pardon the reference, Reverend," he said, turning to the handsome, nervous-looking fifty-five-year-old man at the end of the table.

There was a general murmur of agreement around the room as another man stood up and told of something that had happened in a neighboring city when it had been discovered that one of the pastors had cheated on his income tax and the deacons had let him stay. That church's giving, it seemed, had taken an immediate nose-dive when the word had gotten out.

15

The big man, obviously feeling that everyone was with him now, said, "Listen, I've got a compromise solution. What we can do is tell Bill that if he'll leave quietly, we'll help him get another job and won't tell anybody what's happened. If he won't leave—if he insists on having this public hearing and trial . . ." The big man paused, raised his eyebrows dramatically as he looked around the room, and continued, " . . . we'll hint broadly to him that it might be very difficult for him to get a job—ever."

Although several of the men looked uncomfortable, no one said anything. Finally, the meek-looking man who had spoken up before turned to the pastor and said, "What do you say, Reverend?"

A hush fell over the room. Everyone knew that the minister had hired the education director and had been very close to the younger man and his family.

The minister took off his glasses and looked at the ceiling as he chewed the left earpiece. He was cool now, as if he were stepping into the pulpit. He looked at the other men around the table, cleared his throat, and said in wise and measured tones, "As you know, Bill and I are good friends. I think he's done an excellent job, and I certainly want to be the first to stand by him in every way that I can. But we all know that he and his secretary *do* kid around with each other a lot. I hear them laughing from down the hall several times a day.

"Of course, there's no question that the New Testament condemns fornication, and that adultery is judged even more harshly. And the rumors have already started going around the church. . . .

"The new sanctuary is something I've been preparing this congregation for and praying about night and day for twenty years. As you remember, the vote for it was unanimous, which indicates to me that it is clearly God's will that we build it. And there is a clear New Testament principle that sometimes it is better for one man to suffer rather than the whole people."

He paused for emphasis and then went on. "So, I'm afraid that actually—and for Bill's own good—it might be that we should help him find another place. With deep regret I must agree with our chairman."

I was about to say something when I felt myself again being lifted, and we shot out of the room like a skyrocket going off. I could feel the trembling rage of the Presence.

"Did you hear that?" He said.

I was quiet a few seconds and then answered, "Well, You have to admit You've made it pretty clear that both adultery and fornication are serious offenses."

"But he *didn't do it!*" The Presence almost shouted. "Don't you see, they're supposed to be that man's brothers. But he's not even in the meeting. They didn't call him in to talk it over with him or give him a chance. That secretary of his is so sexually hung up she thinks *everybody* is in love with her. Because he was kind and friendly to her, she developed a fantasy that he was interested in her sexually, and when she found out she was wrong, her pride was so hurt that she accused him. Unfortunately, this isn't the first time this has happened in My church."

"Pardon me, Sir," I said very carefully, "but that sure sounds like a male chauvinist judgment. Are You saying that all sexual problems among Your people are the fault of women?"

The Presence looked at me as if I'd lost my mind. "No," He said, "*of course* I'm not saying that. Anyone who thinks that doesn't understand the human condition or My Word. It happens that in *this particular case* the secretary has some serious emotional problems and accused the minister falsely."

"But," He continued, "what I was trying to point out is that because there are so many instances of *real* sexual infidelity in My church, people tend to jump in and condemn and 'make examples of' those suspected, or to just get rid of them as they are trying to here, without ever bothering to find out what really happened."

"Yeah," I said thoughtfully, "but those deacons don't know all that, and You've got to admit this looked pretty bad. And after all, that poor senior minister has worked for twenty years trying to get those people in shape to commit and build that new sanctuary. Besides, what *about* that New Testament principle concerning the necessity for one man to suffer and die that the good of the whole community might be preserved?"

"Listen Miller, I can't believe you! I thought you had read My book! In the first place, it was Caiaphas, not Jesus, who brought up 'that New Testament principle.' And he used it to try to do away with an *innocent Jesus!* It's very dangerous to use the Scriptures out of context for your own purposes. And besides, after reading My Word for thirty-five years, don't you know that I care more about what happens to that *one young man* and that emotionally troubled secretary than I do about all of the buildings that congregation could build in a hundred years? I didn't command My people to *build buildings;* I commanded them to *love one another!*

"As for those sexual sins—even if the man were guilty, and he's not, those sins are not nearly as bad as hypocrisy and deception. Outright sins can be faced, repented of, confessed, and forgiven. And wisdom and charity can come from the tragedies which have been experienced. But hypocrisy, the willful *covering up* or *denial* of one's sins, removes the sinner from the possibility of My loving correction—from the process of confession leading to forgiveness and Grace-given righteousness. So from My perspective, hypocrisy is a far more deadly spiritual cancer than the obvious sins of the flesh!"

He was getting pretty worked up as He went on, "I thought I made that absolutely clear in the New Testament. I spent ten times as much space dealing with hypocrisy and judgmentalism than all the outward sins put together. And besides, two of those men in that deacon's meeting who voted against the young man have been committing adultery, more or less regularly, for the past fifteen years!"

"Listen, Sir, You're not going to expect me to tell that to Your people, are You? They'll never believe it."

"Whether they believe it or not is not the issue, Keith. It's true. These people who are so quick to condemn their brothers and sisters are often either hiding something themselves, or repressing their own sexuality in an unhealthy way, or secretly wishing they had the guts to sin. And they are going to make sure they stamp out anybody else who steps across the line in a moment of weakness—or anybody who is even accused of it."

"Wait a minute, Sir, are you trying to tell me that this sort of thing is going on all over Your church?"

He looked at me to make sure exactly what I was asking Him. Then He said, "Yes, I am. I'm not saying that there are sexual problems among the clergy and lay leaders in every church, though those kinds of problems are more common than you would dream. But I am saying that I

19

cannot recall *a single church* in which the same kind of compromising of My will to material expediency doesn't happen more or less regularly in the leadership meetings, either visibly or subtly. Don't you see that, whether the issue is accusing a Christian education director of a seduction or getting around the strong-willed head of the women of the church with a 'white' lie, *I hate the hypocrisy and deception* which goes on in all the governing boards in My church!"

3

I was trying to interrupt Him to say once again that I'd really rather He'd pick someone else, when all of a sudden we started diving again. This time we were going down toward an office building in the middle of the business district of another city. A large cloud was moving across the moon, and I could only see part of the plaque on the front of the building: ". . . , Evangelist."

As we hovered outside the window, I could tell there was some sort of a board meeting going on inside. I recognized the man at the end of the table; I'd seen him on TV. Just as we started inside, the Presence whispered, "This one may be a little uncomfortable for you, but I want you to see it."

A man wearing a black suit and dark gray tie was speaking. He wore horned-rimmed half-glasses and was holding in his hands what was obviously a financial report. As we came within the sound of his voice, he was saying ". . . and our revenue has fallen seven thousand dollars a day for the past fourteen days." He put the paper down and looked around the group. Finally his focus came back to the man at the head of the table. "Now the last thing I'd want to do is to suggest that you stop talking about something the Lord has given you to talk about. But I think we've gotta face the fact that, however painful some of these social issues are to you, a lot of our audience just isn't ready to face them. And I think we've got to bring them along slowly, educate them until they are ready to hear the truth about some of these . . ."

I turned to the Presence and whispered, "What does that mean, 'we've got to educate the people' before we can tell them the truth?"

"Nothing, it means absolutely nothing. It's an old Christian copout, often used by ministers and traveling speakers like you, which actually means *the speaker* is afraid to risk telling the people the truth. Those who are afraid to chance telling the truth because of the personal consequences to themselves—or to their vocational success—often claim their *audience* 'isn't ready for it.' This is so common among ministers in local congregations, Sunday school teachers, and traveling Christian speakers that it is almost unbelievable."

"But wait," I interrupted, "in a way they're right! It's true that you can't just vomit the whole truth on people all at once. You *have* to bring people along on some issues so they'll have the background to be able to handle the truth. Remember how Paul said that he was giving the people milk because they couldn't stand meat yet?"

"Yes," the Presence said patiently, "I remember. As a matter of fact, I authored the book you read that in. But Paul went on to give the people meat—*raw meat!*— in Corinth, Rome, Galatia, and he even confronted Peter in Antioch. But all you contemporary Christian leaders seem to do is bring one group along, getting them ready to hear the bald truth, and then the next year start bringing along a new group. You *never* seem to get *any* of them to the place where you dare to confront them with the really hard truths of My gospel. And I'm sick of your using 'the necessity of bringing people along' as an excuse for not eventually telling them the whole truth as you know it in your hearts!"

I was stunned, and I remembered my own hedging on racial and women's issues—long after I knew in my heart that our behavior in the church was shameful in both areas. "Good Lord, You're right," I said in a sort of daze, as He continued.

"And the speakers' rationalizations are so smooth that those doing it are often unaware that their behavior is cowardly. That's one of the things which has made Me so sad for years and which lately has been making Me so angry—the self-deception. Can't you see how inconsistent it is? People will be so jealously particular about keeping the truth of the doctrine 'pure,' but then they will turn around and avoid confronting their constituencies with certain social, political, or even theological issues because the people 'may not be ready' to hear that truth.

"And your more liberal brothers and sisters are often just as afraid to preach the reality of the Incarnation or even use the name 'Jesus' because of this same fear of rejection from their audiences or peers. And yet they all—liberal or conservative—say, and most really believe, that they want to speak the truth."

The Presence turned to look me in the eyes, "That's why I want you to report what I am showing you—

exactly as you are seeing it tonight. Almost everyone will think that either you are suicidal or you believe with all your heart that what you are reporting is My truth."

I shook my head, "But if I tell Your people these things, I know they will say that I am being judgmental, hostile, and simplistic, that I am giving a one-sided picture and leaving out all the wonderful and loving things going on in Your church. And I *know* that there are wonderful things going on out there."

"Yes," He said, "there certainly are some wonderful clergy and lay people who are doing great and loving things in the various denominations and church groups— thousands of quietly faithful men and women. I want you to tell them that I see their struggles to have integrity in the midst of church bodies which sometimes make fun of them or isolate them from the sources of power and money in the church. I have known these faithful ones and known about their sacrifice and about their quiet work for years. And I think they will hear what you tell them and be thrilled that I am confronting My church with its sin. You see, Keith, these 'committed lovers'—ministers and lay persons—are the remnant of My people. And they are the ones who can lead the whole church to new life!"

"But wait," I said, "what about the people outside the church that we are trying to evangelize? Won't my revealing this 'dirty laundry' keep some of them out of the church?"

"No," He said, "I don't think so. Many of the people who are now outside the church left it because they saw that the things you're seeing were going on and no one inside the church seemed to notice. They thought Christians were either hopelessly naïve or just cowardly.

The ones still interested in Me may be thrilled that the church is *facing* its own lack of honesty and integrity."

"But don't You understand?" I said, pleading. "It's considered really bad form for Christians like me who plan to stay in the church to talk openly and publicly about sin and dishonesty among the church's leaders and members—even though I include myself among them. They'll think I'm arrogant . . . and rude . . . and against the church . . . and . . ."

"Go on," He interrupted, "give Me some more good reasons not to tell them."

"What do You mean?" I asked, a little miffed at what I perceived to be His sarcasm.

"Well, Keith, for years these excuses you're giving— about being considered judgmental, simplistic, arrogant, anti-church, and so on—have kept people in the church from doing what I'm asking you to do. You contemporary Christian 'spokespersons' all seem to be more concerned with what people think of you than you are with doing My will."

"But how will I know for *sure* that I'm saying it the right way?"

"You won't."

My mind was filled with pictures of angry faces all glowering at me. I finally blurted out, with what I'm afraid sounded a little like a childish whine in my voice, "But I'm just getting on my feet. My books are beginning to sell well again. Who will justify me when I am accused of exaggerating and giving a one-sided case?"

"I will."

"Oh."

The Presence looked at me with gentleness and understanding and yet said with great firmness, "Do what

I ask you to do, Keith, and leave the other people up to Me. You see, I believe that most of My people will know in their hearts that there is truth in what I am showing you."

My mind was brought back to the conference room by the loud voices, raised in what was evidently a heated argument. The Presence put His finger to His lips.

"Shh, be quiet and listen," He said.

The evangelist I had recognized at the end of the table was clearing his throat and was about to speak when he was interrupted. The new speaker was a well-built man with a bull neck sitting halfway down the table. His coat was off, his sleeves were rolled up almost to his elbow, and his tie was loosened.

"Listen, we can't go off half-cocked here. We've got hundreds of people and a lot of real estate the Lord has given us to look after," he said, gesturing with his hand around the room. Turning to the evangelist, he continued. "If you decide to be a dadgum radical we can't keep this ministry going. And if we don't keep it going, *how are the people going to hear the gospel?* Don't you see, it's not a matter of being afraid to tell the truth. It's simply that our mission is to tell people about the gospel of Jesus Christ—not to solve all of the social and political problems in the world."

He was warming up to his subject: "I'm against war and slums and the mistreatment of minority groups as much as anybody, but I thought I'd die that night two weeks ago when you said on the air that you'd been thinking about it and felt that 'God just might care as much about the homosexuals in that ring the police broke up as he does about the officers who were arresting them.' Or two days later when you took off on abortion . . .

Look, those things may be interesting to you, but my prayer is that you will stick to preaching the Word about Jesus."

Silence hung heavily over the room. I heard a deep sigh coming from the man at the end of the table whose shoulders were bent forward as he shook his head. "Listen," he said, "I'm doing the best I can. And I don't want to say anything that isn't scriptural! But sometimes I think we've created a monster, men. I know what you're saying is true, and that people will only tolerate certain issues being dealt with on the air or they'll quit giving their money. And I also realize that we've hired hundreds of people and that they depend on us for their living. But sometimes I get sick of having to be so careful about what I say. And sometimes it's hard to keep the 'unpopular problems' people are having out in the world separated from the gospel as Jesus talked about it— though the Lord knows I try not to offend our audience.

"It's just that as I get older I'm getting restless about some things. I'm supposed to be 'prophetic' and the leader of this outfit, but sometimes I think I've sold out somehow, that I've become a slave to you and the property of those people out there who can use their giving to control what kind of truth I'm allowed to say."

Someone started to interrupt him and the evangelist held his hand up to stop him. "Let me finish," he said wearily, "I'm going to pray about this. And," he added, turning his palms up, "you know I'm not going to do anything stupid and destroy the ministry."

I was about to say something when suddenly I found myself out in the night air again, about six thousand feet up and still climbing.

"Did you hear that?" the Presence asked. "Those guys

spend half their time studying the audience. They've got members of their team sitting among the people in their evangelistic meetings, listening to comments being made when certain stories are told, so they can find out what 'works' and what doesn't 'work.' I'm not saying all that technique is so bad, but what I really want them to do is to concentrate *on Me* and on *what I'm telling them to say!* My Word is still My Word—even if people won't pay to hear certain parts of it.

"And I'm not saying that they shouldn't make evangelism the main thrust of their message. After all, I invented evangelism in the first place. But Keith, there shouldn't be *any* pain or problem that is 'off limits' for a speaker announcing the Good News of My healing grace to all persons. A lot of My people desperately need to hear that My gospel is more than salvation from a distant hell. They need to hear that the gospel is also a call to love the people in the world who are broken and alienated in *any* way, socially and politically as well as 'spiritually.' As a matter of fact, in the New Testament when I came in the flesh, I made it pretty difficult to separate the 'spiritual' from the rest of life."

"Listen . . . Sir," I interrupted, "it sounds to me like You are beating on conservatives like a liberal would. Are you saying that the liberal Christians are more nearly Your people?"

The Presence threw back His head and laughed, then said, "Oh *no*, Keith, many of them don't even *believe* in Me any more—much less in My Son—and some of them have become amateur sociologists who don't really have any faith in the healing power of My Spirit, except in some vague, symbolic way. No, in the long run a Christian can't do either evangelism or really effective

28

social action—social action that leads to My kind of healing—without a personal relationship with Me.

"But Keith," He said passionately, "I *do* want you Christians to evangelize the world, and I *also* want you to feed the hungry and to takes some risks to be My peacemakers and try to do away with war."

"Wait," I said, "I think a lot of us Christian speakers hesitate to speak about peace and disarmament because we really don't understand the issues, and it would take a lot of research to be prepared to speak out intelligently."

"Well," He said, with what I thought was a slightly mocking smile, "your insurance and retirement plans and your fringe benefits appear to be fairly complex too, but you all seem to be willing to research them." I cringed and knew He was right. And I thought of how often I had used my "lack of knowledge" as an excuse for not facing issues important to Him.

I started to say something, but He had returned to the subject of TV ministries. "I know that their economic dilemma is much more difficult and complex than someone outside the religious television industry might think. But all I can say is that if I call people to preach My Word, they may have to *cut their overhead severely* so they can 'afford' to say the truth as I give it to them."

I turned to the Presence just as we disappeared into a small cloud and reappeared as suddenly. "Sir, I think I understand what You are getting at, but I can promise You that what the people in that room are saying is true— that many of their listeners *are* scared to death of 'liberals' and biblical scholars and sociologists—people like that— and think Christianity should leave the poor, the criminals, and the victims of racial discrimination to the government. Those media ministers *do* have to be careful

29

about expressing compassion for some criminal offenders and mentioning certain politically loaded subjects on the air, because some of these listeners who don't understand will get turned off, and there goes your program! Are You saying that it's better to say the truth all the time, even if it means losing your constituency?"

"Look," He said with a sigh as He shook His head, "I know how hard it is to have integrity. And I know that you are *all going to fail*. That's why I invented confession and forgiveness. But what worries me is that I see so many Christian leaders concentrating on *not* failing, avoiding *any chance* of failure with their audiences. I'm not demanding that these people— including you—be perfect disciples. I just want you all to concentrate on *My message* and to *face* the phony rationalizations you all are engaging in. I want you to take the risk of being as honest as you can, even if you have to lose a certain way of communicating the gospel.

"Keith, don't you understand? I don't *need* a television or radio or publishing ministry! Don't you people know who I *am?* I can still raise up prophets from the stones. And I am a lot more interested in the souls of the evangelists and their teams than I am in their 'saving thousands of people'—*if* they have to bend their integrity to do it. I do not now, nor have I ever, believed that worthy ends justify shoddy or dishonest means!"

"Boy," I said, "I can really hear You! I've been disturbed about dishonesty and self-deception in the church for years. If You have read any of my books, You know . . ."

"Keith," he interrupted, "I can't believe your arrogance. One of the reasons you've never wanted to host one of those television programs is that you were afraid of this very problem—of not being free to say whatever you wanted to. Well, you *don't* have a program. And I want to ask you a question: Have *you* always been honest and courageous and said what I told you to say?"

I felt a sense of shame sweep over me. And to my embarrassment I began to weep. Finally, wiping my eyes with a Kleenex from my pajama shirt pocket, I said, "You know I haven't, Lord. As a matter of fact lots of times when sophisticated strangers ask me what I write about—and I sense they don't have much respect for Christians—I say, 'Well, I've written a lot of books about 'psychology and religion,' because I am ashamed to tell them how much I love You, Lord, and how dear You are to me. In my fear of rejection I want to make myself a little more 'respectable' in their eyes. I'm really ashamed of this, Lord; and if You hadn't come to get me tonight, I'd probably never have admitted that to anyone."

As I realized the awfulness and extent of my denial of Him—which I'd never seen in that light before—I felt nauseated. I remembered, too, how reasonable the arguments of good friends and editors had been about avoiding certain "hard" truths in my own books. I finally said, "I am so sorry about this sin and for the many other ways I have not been honest as I have spoken and written about You and Your message." My heart was in my stomach and I felt an irrational fear sweep over me as I added, "I know how often I have chickened out and that I don't deserve to be forgiven. But . . . will You forgive me?"

"Yes," He said simply, "you are forgiven. And of course you're not alone. I can't think of anybody who doesn't deny Me in one way or another—either outwardly, or in the secrecy of their hearts—even if they are very vociferous about being one of My followers. What really makes Me sad though," He continued, "is to see these great Christian leaders—conservative and liberal—who are so talented and committed to Me, being drawn subtly and unconsciously into putting the financial needs of their organizations first. I'm particularly sad because *eventually* this doublemindedness will erode their integrity and destroy their effectiveness with seeking people—and they will never understand why it happened. I made it quite clear, years ago, that you cannot serve two masters."

As I tried to absorb what had happened, I thought to myself, "No wonder a lot of thinking people with integrity have rejected Christianity. So often, we only deal with those parts of the truth that enhance our reputations with our constituencies—or our friends. And we deceive ourselves by repressing other issues, rationalizing to ourselves that they are unimportant."

We flew on in silence for a few minutes, and I noticed that the blinking stars were so much brighter when we got above all the confusing glare of the man-made lights. Far below, there was only an occasional winking yellow pinpoint from a farmhouse as we flew over the foothills leading to a mountain range ahead.

"Keith," the Presence finally said gently, "why can't you Christians see how much better life is when you're open with each other in love? All of this hiding and pretense just makes you miserable. And in spite of all your rationalization, the failure to disclose who you are doesn't really do any good. You can say all of the 'right Christian words' and all of the beautiful phrases. But if you aren't authentic, somehow the people who are in real pain in the world can 'smell' the unreality, and they steer clear of My church. So what you wind up doing is having meetings and TV programs largely made up of people who are already semi-convinced about the faith, people who actually want you to confirm and bless their own personal (and often unconscious) hiding from the stark truth about themselves and life. And you speakers and leaders propagate this conspiracy by agreeing not to rock the boat about the universal self-deception in the church.

"And yet, even though the people are hiding and scared, somehow at the same time they are haunted by an idea. They yearn for a group of believers to come along—as has happened so often in the past—and to tell the truth to the church, to wake her up like a giant sleeping beauty with a kiss of Reality."

I thought about it a minute and then said, "Lord, I know what You are saying is true. But You did manage to remain totally sinless in Jesus. And I guess it's hard for You to realize just how trapped we *still feel* in our *experience* of sin—even after all You did through the death and resurrection of Jesus—and how afraid we are to speak the naked truth that we see. And it's especially frightening when speaking out might destroy us vocationally.

"Of course, a lot of us who speak for You really do think of ourselves as speaking the truth most of the time. But I think You're right; we Christian leader-types *do* deceive ourselves. We have a sort of unspoken agreement not to tell the kind of bald-faced truth which would make *the people who support us* angry or make them reject us or start gossip campaigns against us. Those of us You have chosen to be Your ministers are so shot through with this kind of unreality that we usually aren't even consciously aware of it.

"I've seen this lack of integrity in other people and in the church for years. And the last few years—to my horror—I have seen it in myself, too. I've tried to bring our dishonesty to people's consciousness through my work. I thought I was doing pretty well . . . until I blew it and failed . . . and . . ."

"Then everybody was really glad they could dismiss you and your call to honesty . . . is that what you're saying?"

"I don't know about that, Lord. All I know is that the last few years I've been sort of hesitant to jump out there and confront *anybody*. Who am I to be telling other people about their failures and problems and dishonesty?"

"For Pete's sake, Keith! When are you going to hear the gospel message that *you are forgiven*—and that I love you as much right now as I did the day you first turned to Me? How many times do I have to tell you My good news that each time you have repented, confessed, asked for forgiveness, and made what restitution you can, you are *completely forgiven*—so completely, in fact, that it is as if you had never sinned at all. I'm simply not going to let you use 'old sins' as a copout to get out of saying what I want you to say. If I had to find a sinless person as My speaker I'd be talking to Myself all day long."

"Okay, Lord," I said, shaking my head, "but sometimes I don't even know what the truth is."

"Well, I can see that. It's been so long since you Christians who call yourselves my people have talked bald-faced truth in love to each other that you're going to have to learn how to do it all over again. But if you'll speak the truth you *do* know in love, I'll show you some more. And after a few years of trying to be open, you'll understand much better which things are true and which things aren't.

"It sounds strange, but that's the way it works. You don't get truth delivered in a pure form like Jesus but once. The rest of the time it's always contaminated by the time you get it. That reminds Me of our next stop. Look out, here we go."

4

As we flew through the night I could see that the moon had changed positions and was nearly halfway across the sky. I was marveling at how vast and distant the Milky Way was. Then, while I was stargazing, we suddenly began to tumble over and over. I hollered, "Help!" and clamped my eyes shut. The Presence laughed and said, "I was talking to you and you weren't listening."

"I'm listening now," I said, feeling my heart racing inside my pajama shirt.

"Besides, I needed to do those circles because we're going to do something a little different now. I needed you to close your eyes . . ."

When I opened my eyes again I saw that it was suddenly broad daylight. As a matter of fact, it was about two minutes until eleven according to the town clock we were approaching very rapidly.

As we sneaked quietly into the back pew of a stately gothic church with a narrow nave and lovely stained glass windows, I noticed a beautiful polished cross on the altar and elegant candelabra on either side of it.

The congregation was singing a hymn. At first I thought we had come into a funeral. Then I recognized we were in a Sunday morning worship service in my own denomination. After a few minutes of embarrassment at the dragging, listless singing, I whispered to the Presence rather apologetically that most of our people didn't have a lot of training in music.

"Don't give me that hogwash," He said. "Unfortunately, you people don't have a patent on bad singing. Only a few churches do it really well, and some of those take such pride in it that they spoil it for Me.

"No, there are a couple of very good reasons besides 'lack of training' for the fact that Christians don't sing in the worship services. In the first place, they're not happy. Happy people are those who've just received forgiveness and new hope. And it takes *confession* to experience forgiveness. Many of the people in your church don't even confess anymore, except in some general sort of way, so it's no wonder they're not grateful. The experience of forgiveness is the main thing that has always made Christians so joyful.

"But there's another thing, too," He said. "Look over there." He pointed toward a young woman who was singing as if she really meant it.

When the words "hallelujah, hallelujah" came, this woman really sang out—not ostentatiously but with honest and obvious joy. An older lady in a fur stole sitting in front of her turned around and gave the younger woman a hostile glare that was apparently intended to stop the "awful" volume and "crudeness." The young woman stopped and looked at her for a second, computed what she meant, and then, without the slightest sign of rudeness, went right on singing. But then two other people in the front row turned around and stared at her, and at last she muted her voice.

"*That's* the other reason people don't sing joyously in church," the Presence whispered to me. "Most Christians are far more interested in being considered moderate and having 'good taste' than in worshiping Me with anything approaching 'joyful abandon.' "

The congregation was now droning through the prayer book service. Almost everyone was reading in a dull monotone. But the minister read with a loud, clear voice. Although he seemed to be very sincere, I had the distinct impression that he was performing the function of a steel rabbit at the dog races—to get the congregation through the liturgy a little faster.

When it was time for communion, the Presence excused Himself and went up to the altar at the front of the church. I guess I was the only one who could see Him. As each person received the bread and wine, He reached right inside and touched his or her heart—if they opened it to Him. Then He returned to me as the people were coming back to their pews, and He whispered, "Let's go outside. There's a meeting right after the service I want to make."

As we stood in the yard waiting for the people to come out, I asked, "Aren't You discouraged by all of that monotone reading of the liturgy?"

"Yes," He said, "I'd be thrilled if more people thought about what they were saying and really put themselves into it as if it were a drama instead of a dirge. But the best thing about that whole service is that it points the people to Me, and the thing that saves it is that there is a place in it for us to meet and touch each other. That's what I invented the sacrament of the bread and wine

38

for—so that people would have a sense of taking Me into their bloodstream, into their lives where they really live. I chose common elements to which everyone has access so you could all see that you can take My Spirit into your lives as easily as you take in food or water. So even if the sermon is boring and inept and people's minds drift off during the reading of the service, there is a 'place' in the liturgy for us to meet and for Me to come in and touch your hearts and give you the forgiveness and the joy you can't get anywhere else."

"What about churches which don't look at communion that way?" I asked.

"Well," He said slowly, "every church which is still around has *some* central channel in its worship service through which I can touch peoples' hearts. With some it's preaching—though it's tough, even for Me, to come through *some* of those sermons. And sometimes it's the music or the prayer or the reading of My Word. But if there is no definite, regular way for Me to meet each person in the worship service, that church just doesn't last long as one of Mine."

"What do You mean by that?"

He looked off in the distance and then said, "Such 'churches' look like Christian churches on the outside. But if there's no place in their worship for regular living contact with Me, then they become psychological or sociological centers or historical societies in disguise— with an occasional nod to My Word or sacraments. If the ministers and people don't experience Me as being alive in their worship, then they have shut Me out of their community, whether they know it or not. And this sterile corporate plague has swept across several major denominations and evangelical groups in the past, leaving a spiritual wasteland which only has the faintest memory-trace of being a joyful outpost of My kingdom."

Now the people were coming out all around us. The Presence excused Himself and went over to talk to the young woman who had been singing with such a joyful and enthusiastic voice. Although she couldn't see Him, she knew He was there, and she smiled at the next person who came out of the church as if he were the Presence himself.

When the Presence came back over where I was, He said, "That's one of My special ones. She'll go through a lot of pain while she's here because her faith is so pure and because she really believes I should be Lord in every area of her life, in every relationship. But even though she'll have to cry a lot, she's going to wind up being very happy in her inner life; and she's not afraid very often because she knows I'm always within earshot."

As the people drifted away toward their cars, we ducked into a meeting room with a long walnut table— very much like an executive conference room in a business. The senior warden was calling the group to order and asked the minister to begin with a prayer. By the looks of the people involved, the gathering could have been the board meeting of an important bank. And the senior warden was a calm but powerful presence in the room.

It turned out that the minister had a special request on his mind. He'd been troubled for months, he said, about the recent change in the economic conditions in their community and about the numbers of people who were virtually starving all around them. And three nights before he'd had what he considered to be a clear indication from God that the parish should take the lead in alleviating the suffering in their city. But it would take real sacrifice on the part of the congregation.

He stopped and then went on, "I've told our senior warden about this, but now I'm asking you to consider giving an amount equal to a quarter of our annual budget for the feeding of the hungry people who are jobless in our area."

He went on to give such an impassioned, honest, and straightforward plea that I almost stepped forward and cheered. And I probably would have if the Presence hadn't tugged at my sleeve and with His finger to His mouth told me to be quiet. I was really proud of being a member of that denomination and smiled my approval at the Presence.

He just whispered, "Keep listening." When the minister had finished his presentation and sat down, there was silence. He had suggested ways in which the existing budget could be cut, including postponing the raise which had been promised to him. Finally, the lone woman on the vestry said, "In good conscience I don't think we can do anything else except what you suggest. It is obviously a crucial and pressing need. As treasurer I can tell you that it'll be a real sacrifice to us because there's a shortfall in our pledge income this month. But I think that if we all get out and present this to the parish by making some individual calls, we'll be able to put it across." Silence.

The senior warden stood and cleared his throat "Does anybody else have anything to say?" No one spoke. "Do I hear a motion?" Silence.

The woman looked around, confused, but finally said, "I move that we accept the rector's suggestion and allocate the money for feeding the poor."

"Is there a second?" the senior warden asked. Silence. Finally the minister said, "Second."

"All in favor, raise your hand" (from the senior warden).

I was smiling in anticipation when, to my horror, only two hands went up, the woman's and the rector's.

"Well then," the senior warden said, "If there is no further business. . . ."

"*Wait* a minute," the woman said, "maybe we ought to stop and ask what God would want us to do about the poor!"

"Who?" the senior warden asked.

"*God*" the woman replied angrily. "You know, the one who *owns* the place!" And she gestured with her hand to indicate the building they were in.

But everyone in the room except the minister either looked down at the table top or avoided the woman's eyes in other directions. It appeared for a moment that the minister was going to confront the senior warden. But after looking at him a few seconds, the minister's eyes dropped to the table, too, and he didn't say anything either.

I stepped forward and said, "Wait, I've got to . . ."

Suddenly I was high in the sky, tumbling over and over with my eyes closed. When I opened them it was night again. "Why did you take me away? There was something wrong going on down there. There was a mistake. Those vestrymen didn't understand."

The Presence shook His head. "No, Keith, they understood."

"What happened, then?"

"Well," He said sadly, "the senior warden informally invited most of the vestry members over to his house

42

last night—all except the minister and the woman. They sat around and drank coffee and decided they were going to defeat the minister's plan because it was going to 'put a strain on the church's already-taxed budget.' Besides, as the senior warden pointed out, his wife had told him that the women of the church are going to need a lot more seed money for the decorations at the bazaar this year because they want to use an elaborate circus motif."

I laughed, *"A circus motif?* The whole thing sounds crazy," I said, shaking my head, "I thought the *purpose* of a church bazaar was to raise money to help the poor. But the senior warden is taking the money *away from* the needy who are hungry *now*—so the ladies can enjoy making some money to help someone at the end of the year!"

"That's right," the Presence said, raising His eyebrows and nodding His head.

"But the secret meeting—the whole thing—is *dishonest,"* I said.

"Yes, Keith, I know it's dishonest."

I was quiet for a few seconds, and then asked, "Why didn't someone support the woman in challenging the big man leading the group—the senior warden?"

"Because they are afraid of him. He's a banker and very wealthy. He gives the minister a free membership to his health club every year, and he knows the financial secrets of almost everyone in the room."

"But if the minister puts that financial hook above his principles, the banker has in effect bought his soul."

"That's right, Keith, and in different ways it's happening to certain ministers all over My church— though the ministers involved would be furious if anyone suggested that.

43

"Of course, there's nothing wrong with lay people helping ministers financially like that—if the 'helper' doesn't expect (or isn't offered) fealty in return. And there's certainly nothing wrong with Christians being wealthy—some of My most generous, committed, and loving people are financially well off. But the tragedy is that in many cases financially powerful people with a nominal faith control a church's decisions—with a very worldly power and know-how, and almost without regard to My gospel or My Spirit."

"That's terrible!" I said, "What can be done to stop this?"

The Presence shook His head and thought a minute. Then He said, "The answer is simple, but the risk involved makes it incredibly hard for ministers to try it. All the church would have to do to stop this 'control' would be for the minister and the people to decide to say no to these powerful men and women and vote them out of office. But they would have to be ready for the powerful people to take their money and go to another church. And other members may follow the powerful people out of the church if the minister begins to stand up to them and speak honestly and courageously about his or her feelings and convictions.

"On the other hand, the powerful 'lay pope' figure may go behind the minister's back and get him removed. That happens enough times to cause ministers who are considering this course to think twice. Unfortunately, we don't have a lot of contemporary records on what happens when a 'successful' minister decides to stand firm against such financial and social pressures—not that many have tried it! But the good news is that some of those who *have* tried it with a small group of deeply committed people have discovered that after a while new members will come. They will replace the old materialist power players and bring new life and greater overall giving. And renewal will have crept into that congregation's life.

"But," the Presence continued, "the tragedy from My perspective is that too many of My ministers seem to be more interested in associating with the socially and economically powerful families in their communities than in calling the church to renewal. And very few of them are willing to risk losing the good will of such folk in their congregations—even to have new life in the church."

"Why is it so hard," I asked, "for them to risk being honest with such people?"

He looked at me and said, smiling, "Think back to when you were working for a major corporation."

"Okay."

"Did you always confront your boss when he was being overbearing and seemed to be wrong?"

"Oh," I said, "I see what You mean." And I remembered how hard it always was for me to risk my job, even when I felt some company policies and officials were wrong or even dishonest.

"Yes," the Presence continued, "I can understand why it is so frightening to confront people in a materialist institution. But the *church* was never meant to be like other institutions with power players at the head. It was supposed to be a *family* with Me as the head. And yet My people have often given the 'Father's place' in My family to powerful lay persons—or clergy. But there can never be authentic Christianity in the church until this control is taken out of the hands of these lay or clergy autocrats—who may be sincere but whose lives are often unconverted—and given back to Me. I am getting very discouraged and angry that virtually no one will risk doing this. Almost everywhere I look, my church has become a place for playing a sort of 'spiritual croquet' or 'social lawn tennis' with very little passion or commitment. The way that minister got 'handled' in that last vestry meeting was a perfect example of how some powerful people manipulate many situations in My church."

"But that attack was not only aimed at the minister," I said quickly. "It was a perfect example of male chauvinism—leaving the woman out of the secret meeting. I thought we'd gotten past male chauvinism in the church."

The Presence just looked at me as if He couldn't believe my naïveté, as He said, "Come on, Keith, you have only *scratched the surface* of sexual *and racial* discrimination in the church."

I must have looked puzzled, because He went on, "If you don't believe that, ask the women and the members of minority groups who are trying to work on an equal basis with Caucasian men. The church has come a long way, but most of My people don't really see how deep the problems of prejudice are in the church—unless they are members of a group at whom the prejudice is directed. No, you in the church have just begun. *Much* more needs to be done."

"Now I'm ashamed to be a member of that denomination," I said, wanting to cry.

"Don't be ashamed of being a member of that denomination, Keith. There are thousands of wonderful people in your denomination. As you know, they are taking the leadership in feeding hundreds of people in different places right now and in trying to deal with all kinds of discrimination, although even they are just barely beginning from My perspective.

"No, it's not just this denomination. Unfortunately, the same kind of dishonest manipulation we saw here happens in *every* denomination or group of churches in one way or another. Instead of openly confessing to one another their fears about spending too much money or about putting on new programs, people politic behind the minister's back (or with the minister behind everybody else's back). Sometimes the minister stacks the vote or withholds information which might not be favorable to his point of view. I know it sounds incredible, but it happens every day in a church somewhere." He stopped, seeing that I was very disturbed by this whole conversation.

"Well, why don't You help them," I blurted out, "tell them what to do."

"I'd love to help them if they would ask Me," He said sadly. "But in many meetings of the leadership of the church, people are actually embarrassed to say, 'Let's stop and pray about it,' or even to sit in silence and try to listen for My voice. They are embarrassed for people to know they may believe I am *really* with them in the room in My Spirit. It's no wonder there's so much unreality in the church.

"As you well know," He continued, "people like the senior warden we saw are often elected to leadership positions because of their wealth, secular power, and influence—and not at all because of their commitment to Me. Some ministers even *invite* outstanding but unconverted leaders in their communities to come into the church 'to help us,' thinking that this is a good way to evangelize such people. But such an invitation is often interpreted by the 'invited' leader as an honest invitation to help lead or run the church. So he or she comes in and does just that, in the only way he or she knows how—by the nonspiritual rules of secular power. And it never occurs to such people that they are to wait for Me to reveal My will in the community."

He shook His head sadly as He went on talking. "This sort of leadership selection process happens to some degree almost everywhere, especially in large churches. And I keep being amazed at how seldom elders, deacons, sessions, and vestries actually count on *My* power or My presence to get things done. I watch, heartbroken, as they go strictly 'by the numbers' the way they do in their businesses. Some ministers even think of themselves as 'chief executive officers' in a corporation. It makes Me sick, and as I told you it's beginning to make Me *very angry!* As a matter of fact, sometimes lately I've been tempted to call down those thirty-six thousand angels Jesus was talking about in Gethsemane—and just clean the church out and start all over."

"Excuse me, Sir . . . I don't want to be presumptuous, but aren't You supposed to be loving, and aren't You always supposed to forgive?"

"OF COURSE I'm loving!" He practically shouted, and then continued in a hoarse whisper, "but don't you know that loving is *painful,* and that forgiveness isn't just an 'automatic transaction'? It *always costs something to forgive!* Sin is painful to Me—*every time!* Do you think it's easy to promise to forgive people, even when they blaspheme and lie about Me and are hypocritical and impervious to My love and . . . (He looked very sad) . . . and ignore Me?" I thought I saw a tear in His eye.

"Oh, I'm sorry," I said. "I didn't realize."

"No," He said. "People don't. Sometimes I look at the church and the way things are being done, and I wish I hadn't started the whole thing. It is so far from what I had in mind. And yet, as strange as it seems, because I gave all of you freedom, I feel I've got to put up with the results."

He stopped and looked at me, noticing that I was very upset about what He had told me. And He said gently, "I know this is pretty hard on you, having to see all of this, but imagine My feelings, having to see it all the time."

"Please," I said hopefully, "You told me there were some good things going on in Your church. Why don't you show me some of those to tell people about?" (I knew people responded better to bad news if there was some good news included.)

"Listen, Keith, when you are giving a patient a diagnosis for cancer, that's not the time to compliment him on how nice he has kept his complexion or what good shape his muscles are in." I nodded my head as He went on, "As I told you earlier, My Spirit is alive and well among some of My people. But don't worry about the disapproval of those loving and committed men and women when you report what you've seen tonight; they probably feel the same way I do about the things I'm showing you. The tragedy is that *everything you are seeing is actually occurring* somewhere among the churches that are operating today with My name on them."

5

The Presence kept talking, but I couldn't hear the rest
of what He said because the wind was whistling so loudly
in my ears. Then we were zooming down again. Before
I knew it, we had breezed into a room where about twenty
people were having a prayer meeting. One woman was
standing speaking to the rest, and we listened as she
talked.

". . . I just want to praise the Lord for all of the good
things He's given me. Life is such a *joy* since I met Him
and everything is *simply wonderful!* The kids are
wonderful! Frank and I are madly in love again! He's
gotten a raise, so our financial worries are not so great.
Everything is *just perfect!*"

"Well," I whispered to the Presence, *"that* ought to
make You happy. That woman is just filled with love
and joy."

He looked at me with raised eyebrows and whispered,
"She sounds great, but she doesn't *smell* very good."

"What do you mean?"

"Shh," the Presence said. "Listen."

The first woman sat down and then a second began to speak. "I don't know what's the matter with me," she said sadly. "I gave my life to Jesus Christ, too, but sometimes I'm miserable. I'm discovering so many things I don't do that I know are His will. And instead of getting a raise, I lost my job. Yet I love God very much and am finding a great deal of strength through this rough time in my life. You all seem to have it so easy since you've met Jesus, but I find life terribly hard. I'm happy, and strangely my life is filled with a kind of hope and satisfaction I've never known. But things surely aren't easy."

There was an uneasy silence. Then the woman who had lost her job said quietly to the woman with the "perfect" life, "Jane, are you truly *that* happy . . . *all* the time? I really want to know, because I feel like somehow I must have an inadequate faith since I'm not as happy as you are."

Jane was folding a Kleenex into a small square bundle. She watched herself doing this for a few seconds and then looked up. I could see tears glazing her eyes as she said finally, "Ann . . . I, uh, *no,* I'm really *miserable* right now." And she began to cry. "I feel like I'm supposed to be joyful for the Lord because that's what it says I'm supposed to do in the Bible. I try to smile and be happy, and most of the time I can show a happy face. But I have a lot of problems I'm struggling with right now. I don't feel like Frank really understands my new faith. And one of my kids is in real trouble with drugs and won't talk to me. Sometimes I get so desperate I wonder if the whole Christian thing is untrue, or if maybe I didn't really say the right thing at conversion and maybe there's something else I ought to do.

"A year ago I got depressed about this same problem and some friends said I needed to be filled with the Holy Spirit and receive the gift of tongues. They laid hands on me and I did receive the gift. And everything was better for a while. But now I find—when I am really honest with myself—that I still have problems and doubts."

As Jane talked, I felt a warmth and love seep into the room. And I felt a lot of love and caring reaching out to her as she confessed her true condition to those women with whom she had been praying so "joyously" over the months. Ann got up, walked across the circle, and lifted Jane's hands until she stood up. She looked into Jane's eyes and then gave her a warm hug. "Thank you, Jane, you've really helped me. I couldn't relate to all your 'total joyousness' when I knew something about your family situation. But the fact that you have problems like I have, even with your strong faith, somehow makes me stronger. When all you appeared to have was 'joy' and wouldn't tell us about the other part, you seemed phony. Now I know you're not."

There was a tug at my sleeve and I knew it was time to leave. As we soared up through the predawn blackness I couldn't help asking, "What went on down there? I don't understand it. You say You are the source of joy and happiness. And yet, when that first woman—Jane— tried to *project* joy, the room was filled with uneasiness, unreality, and closedness. Then, when Ann spoke, even though *she felt* she was inadequate and didn't have much joy, the room started to fill with happiness. Finally, when Jane admitted that she has problems too, *everybody* got happy all of a sudden, and a sense of peace and love filled the whole room. Why was that?"

The Presence smiled, "Well, Keith, that's the secret, the mystery, of *real* joy. People who are with Me don't have to be afraid to face the pain of life. At a deep—often unconscious—level, everyone is terrified of failure, pain, and death; and they try to avoid these things with everything from tranquilizers to 'religious' meetings. But only when a person has the courage, through faith, to *face* the fears and doubts and pain of life and to *confess* these things—only then can he or she find the doorway to *authentic* joy and to Life."

The Presence smiled as though He were telling me a special secret. He continued, "There is something about the way I made you human beings that many people are not aware of: The small doorway through which joy comes into your hearts is the *same* doorway through which pain and doubt come. That may seem strange to you, but if you block out the pain and doubt and pretend they don't exist, you block out the joy, too.

"The secret is to let the pain and doubt and the joy *all* come into your consciousness and to receive them, claim them, and offer them to Me. When you do that, I can take the pain and doubt and joy of your lives and weave them together into that wonderful, mystical fabric which is the Joy of Christ. And you don't try to *project* My kind of joy, Keith. It's a byproduct, like the scent from a flower."

6

The Presence stopped talking and circled back over a large city we had almost passed by. "Look out, here we go," He said as we went into an almost vertical dive.

This time we were descending toward a large convention center. We floated into a big auditorium filled with what must have been a thousand or fifteen hundred people. Above the stage was a large banner that read, "Christian Radio Convention."

The man at the podium was admonishing the audience, and he was almost at a fever pitch. We stood against the back wall, right in the midst of the overflow crowd.

Then, although the speaker did not appear to be talking on the subject of "the Christian family," he suddenly said, "If you want to strike an effective blow to help protect the Christian family, then **quit** letting these divorced Christian leaders and authors speak on your talk shows! I think it's time we stopped letting divorced people try to teach us *anything* about the gospel— particularly concerning marriage and family!" A great round of applause went through the audience.

Some near the front even stood and applauded.

"Hey," I whispered to the Presence, "that's sort of like instructing a group of sailors not to let a captain who's been shipwrecked in a tricky part of the ocean come back and tell them how you might avoid the hidden obstacles they can't see from shore."

"Yes," the Presence whispered, "it's so strange that they forget it's often been the great sinners like Paul and Augustine who, after they saw their sin, have been able to teach people the most about dealing with sin."

"Come on, there's something else I want you to see," He said. We left the building, going out through an upstairs window. Looking down, I saw a woman sitting on the front steps by herself, her face buried in her hands. She was alone and seemed to be crying her heart out. I pointed as we went by.

"What's the matter with that woman?" I said.

"Well, she just walked out of the meeting in there"— the Presence nodded back over His shoulder. "You see, she came home recently and found on the kitchen table a note from her husband which said he was leaving her. He didn't even leave a forwarding address. Since then she's been trying to run a house and take care of four kids alone. And not only has she been fired from her job as a Christian radio broadcaster for being divorced; she's also been kicked off the Christian Education Board at her church—after twenty-two years of being one of the key teachers in that congregation."

The Presence was silent for a few seconds and finally shook His head and said, "The only actual 'crime' she seems to have committed was that she came home and found the note. The fact that he left her and ran off with another woman doesn't seem to have anything to do with the judgment they put on *her.*"

The Presence shook His head sadly. "You know, I

invented this whole game of life. But if it weren't for the fact that Satan's alive and working, I don't think even *I'd* be able to understand the kind of legalistic, judgmental attitude some of My people have taken in the name of My gospel."

"Wait a minute," I said, trying to sort out what he was saying. "I've always felt that divorce *is* the basic issue in the disintegration of the Christian family."

"No," the Presence said sadly. "Sin—not divorce—is the real threat to the family . . . and to the church. Divorce is a symptom and result of sin. And I made it clear in the Bible that there are ways to deal with sin! If both parties in a Christian marriage which is in trouble would get honest with each other, face and confess their sins and hurts, and get outside counseling help if they need it, many hundreds of divorces between Christians could be avoided. Hiding the problems has never made or redeemed a good Christian marriage.

"And when a divorce does occur—although it breaks My heart—My channels of forgiveness and reconciliation are still open for the people involved. When they repent of their sin, confess it, and ask My forgiveness, I forgive them completely. They don't become 'second-class Christians' in My sight. And many of them can actually teach and lead in new and more effective ways because of what they've learned from the pain and loneliness that sin has caused them."

"You mean," I said slowly, "the way You used Peter as a key leader in Your church after he had sinned and denied You three times—although he'd followed You several years and should have known better?"

The Presence put His forefinger on His chin and thought a few seconds. Then He answered, "Yes, that's the same principle. But, Keith," He want on, "I *do* hate sin, and I hate divorce. I don't want you or anyone to misunderstand that. Yet—*far more important*—I want you to tell My people again that *no* such sin is too great to be forgiven, *no* first failure is too great to be given a second chance. Legalistic people have taken My Word and used it as a whipping instrument until I am sick to death of it."

He rubbed His hand back over His forehead and shook His head as He continued, "I'm sure you'll remember that in the New Testament I said the whole law could be summed up in loving Me with all of your heart and soul and loving your neighbor as yourself. And the new commandment I gave all of you was not 'thou shalt keep the law better than anybody else ever has' (as Saul and many of the Pharisees actually did). Rather, I commanded you to 'love one another.' I want you to keep the law, and I don't ever want you to think otherwise. But having said that, I want you to understand that what I desire most deeply in My heart is for all of you to love each other, to forgive each other, to build each other up, and to *help each other become more responsible to your commitments through love and forgiveness!* Far from wanting to destroy the repentent sinners or discredit them, I want to put a new robe on them and have a party for them as I did in the story of the Prodigal Son. I wonder if people have thought about doing that for those who are divorced or who have been crushed by their own sin or by the sin of others? That's what the story of the Prodigal Son is all about."

I was quiet for a moment, deciding whether or not to ask a question that His comments had triggered. Then I plunged into it: "You know, Sir, in the Old Testament the Ten Commandments are pretty clear. But sometimes I don't understand the laws You gave us in the New Testament. They don't seem to cover a lot of the situations with which life confronts us."

"Well," He said, shaking His head slowly, "that question opens a real can of worms. But I guess I might as well face it with you now, since I'm sending you out to tell My people some very difficult truths.

"You see, I never intended My story in the New Testament to be a 'book of laws.' It's a drama filled with parables and narrative stories about Me and My Kingdom. And what many people don't realize is that in each parable or narrative I was only trying to make *one* point. When you try to make a parable or a story into an analogy that fits at all points, you are misunderstanding the nature of the way truth was conveyed by Jesus as a Hebrew.

"In the same way, when I was addressing a specific situation in which sin was being committed, I wasn't trying to set down new *laws*. I was trying to show, in vivid terms My listeners could grasp, how I would respond to the error being committed. For instance, when I was talking about divorce, I was speaking to the Pharisees, who—at that time—could legally dismiss their wives practically by handing them a handkerchief. They could break women's hearts and break up homes at a whim.

"I told them that marriage relationships do not work that way. I was saying that there really wasn't any excuse for getting a divorce—except possibly if their mate committed adultery. And I hoped their marriages could even survive that. But I tried to make it clear that if they *did* kick their wife out on some pretext and get divorced so they could play around sexually or marry someone else, they were just as much adulterers as if they had never left their first mate.

"What people have done is pulled that admonition out as a universal prohibition for all time: they extrapolate from that teaching situation a law to be applied without exception. And then they claim that in My eyes there is no forgiveness for divorce or that I can't give people new beginnings under certain circumstances if I choose to. See how ridiculous that is? It would limit My power to forgive and to give people creative new starts—which is what the whole New Testament is about."

He raised His eyebrows, and looked at me to see if I understood. Evidently I was looking a little skeptical and confused. So He continued, "Listen once more, Keith: *I hate divorce!* I hate anything that breaks relationships, especially family relationships. But the thing that the New Testament is really filled with is My hatred of hypocrisy. And let Me tell you something, and make no mistake about it: *Self-righteous Christians who will not face their own sins and selfishness are in far greater danger of My disapproval than anyone who has had a divorce and faced his or her sin, confessed it, and made a new beginning in me!*"

"Good Lord," I said. "You don't expect me to say *that*, do You?"

"Of course I do. Somebody's got to say it. It's the truth. And the whole New Testament is permeated with that message."

"Well," I said shaking my head, "a lot of people in Your church sure don't understand it that way!"

"That's why I want you to tell them," He said grimly.

I thought about the reaction people in the church might have to my saying some of the things I had just heard, and I groaned. My uneasiness increased, until I couldn't stand to keep quiet. I took a deep breath.

"I'm *not going to do it!*" I almost shouted. "You know I've gone through a divorce!" My head felt as if there were a steel band around my forehead. And then without warning I felt hot choking tears welling up from somewhere deep within me. "Look, Lord, I know I'm a sinner, and I've faced that with You in spades. But I also know a little about Your people. And I know that if I say these things about divorce, many of them will dismiss everything else You've been showing me tonight, because they'll think this is just a way to justify myself. And . . . I'm just not willing to take that risk!" I shook my head as I took another deep breath and wiped my eyes with my sleeve.

The Presence looked at me and asked evenly, "Even to help helpless and hurting divorced people the church is condemning and rejecting every day in My name? And it's not just divorced people who are hurt by My people's judgment and lack of love and understanding. In many of the most prestigious churches people come in off the street hoping to find My love and acceptance. But the members often shunt aside and ignore the poor, the unusual, the untalented, and the unattractive people who sit down beside them in the pews—the very people I indicated in the Bible I feel closest to. And I want you to speak for them, too."

I wanted to shout again at the Presence—to tell Him to take me home and forget trying to help the Christians who are being crippled by the church's insensitivity and sin. But as I thought these words, I saw that the real issue I was facing in not wanting to tell the people these things was my own awful pride and fear of being misunderstood and rejected.

The Presence put His hand on my shoulder. "Keith," He said gently, "If you report this conversation accurately, most people will have only two ways to respond: They will either understand that you are trying to report what you honestly believe you have heard Me say about these things, or they will think that you are the biggest self-justifying phony in the world. But either way, I promise to be with you."

I shook my head and mumbled under my breath as we passed a flock of high-flying geese. I felt like a small, scared little boy. And I tried to think of other things. I watched the beautiful view as we flew over a deep canyon threaded with a silver river in the moonlight. But I could not get my mind away from the broad implications of what we had been talking about earlier.

7

The Presence started to hum "Amazing Grace" as we flew on through the beautiful moonlit night.

"Wait," I said, "please don't quit talking now. I have something I want to ask You. When You make statements like You've been making, You seem to be saying that laws and rules aren't important. Is that what You mean?"

"Oh *no*," He said quickly, "but it's a paradox. Through Jesus I said that I hadn't come to *destroy* the law but to *fulfill* it. What that meant to Me was that for My people laws are important, but only as structure, not as ends in themselves. Remember when I said that the Sabbath was made to help man, not man to serve the Sabbath? That would be true with regard to *any* of My laws and rules. For example, men and women are not made to 'serve the law' concerning divorce; the prohibition of divorce is made to help structure society and to help keep men and women in families so they can work out their problems together and not run away from them.

"But when the serving of the law or a goal becomes

an end more important than loving people, then any law or even any Christian goal can turn into an evil thing. Keith, that's a cardinal spiritual principle, the ignoring of which has caused Me more pain than you can imagine. Even good things can be twisted to become harmful or evil. For instance, if a person's *ministry* becomes the central focus of his or her life (instead of loving Me and loving other people and trying to do My will), then that ministry can become very destructive, even if the minister isn't 'breaking any law.' In the interest of having that ministry succeed, evil things can be done—like putting the three-million-dollar building fund ahead of loving the education director in that first church we visited tonight.

"What I'm saying is that I want you and all My people to commit your lives to Me and to loving each other. And then I want you to try to determine My will through reading the Scriptures, through prayer, through corporate worship, through the sacraments, through talking together openly and confessing your sins as well as your hopes and dreams.

"All of these things," He continued, "including My Word and the rules and prohibitions in the Bible, have been given to *serve* you and to *help* you to *live and love and participate in My will in the world!* You're supposed to do all of these things the best you can.

"But there's a problem here: *I know that every one of you will fail!* (Not that you *have* to fail, but because of sin it seems inevitable that you *do* fail.) That's what the provision for forgiveness is all about. I forgive you because I know that you will fail, and because I love you and want to bring you back into freedom and a close relationship to Me. And that's what 'Grace' means.

Because you *all* break My commandments, *none* of you deserves new starts. But I give you new chances because I love you and am committed to your spiritual growth and happiness."

"Hmmm, this whole thing is getting to seem awfully difficult to me," I said. "It's not nearly as 'tidy' as it was a few hours ago. How can I take the law seriously and be *just* on one hand, and on the other hand be *loving and forgiving* to other people? For instance, if someone sins according to the law, they've *got* to be held accountable—or the rules become meaningless. On the other hand, You're telling me now that we've *got* to be loving and forgiving, and that that's more important than all of the rules. How can I do both—be genuinely loving and forgiving in the face of specific sin, and still have integrity in regard to the rules?"

He thought about what I'd said. Then He answered, "Well, let Me give you an example from very familiar ground. Think back to the time, years ago, when your children were very young. Let's say that while you were at the office one day two of them went in the kitchen independently of each other and each one stole a cookie—which was against the rules at your house. And let's say the punishment for stealing a cookie was a paddling. Now, one of these two children has stolen the cookie because she feels the need for more attention from you; she knows that if she steals a cookie and gets caught you'll probably paddle her bottom, but that you'll also hold her and spend some time with her, right?"

"Right," I said.

"But your other little girl also steals a cookie. Now, this child is trying to test you to see whether or not she can control you. She steals a cookie and leaves some crumbs on her mouth in an arrogant way, trying to push you to the limit.

"So you've got the same 'crime' committed by both children—cookie stealing, which the 'law' at your house says clearly is punishable by a paddling from Father. Now, you walk into the house, and in one hand you have love and forgiveness, while in the other hand you have righteous judgment. Which one do you use?"

He continued, "If you are doing justice the way *I do it,* you would probably go to the first child and find out what happened. You talk to the child, and you listen to what is beneath her answers. And because you know and love your child so well, you suddenly realize that *this* child needs to be held—that was why she stole the cookie. And you use that occasion to tell her 'you don't have to steal a cookie to get me to pay attention to you; just come and talk to me. I love you and I want to give you my love and attention.' You may paddle her or you may not. But in any case you will hold that child in your arms and spend some time talking to her.

"Now, you come to the other child—the arrogant one who stole the cookie to test her limits. You talk to her, too, and find out what happened and why she broke the rule, and you also know *that* child well. You will probably give *that* child a paddling she'll remember. And then you hold her and tell her there are certain limits in this world, that she has to stay within them. And you say, 'This is what it's like when you don't obey the rules. You get hurt.'

"Now, if you were a legalistic person who was oriented *only* toward righteousness, you would have paddled both children the same way, with no concern as to why they stole the cookies, because they both committed the same 'crime.' You wouldn't pay any attention to why the 'crime' happened and what it meant in the life of the 'criminal.' And you would justify your actions by saying, 'The crime deserves the punishment.'

"On the other hand," He continued, "if you were *only* loving and forgiving—and not righteous and just—you would have forgiven both children without regard to *any* rule. And that would still be ignoring why the crime was committed and what it meant in the life of the child.

"Do you see how it works?" He asked. "I have given you, as a Christian, the enormous responsibility of personally bringing *both* the absolute justice *and* the total love of Jesus Christ into the concrete situations around you in the world. And in each situation *you* must decide how to blend My justice and love to best *cure the brokenness of the person* committing the sin. The purpose of My kind of judgment is to lead those involved toward a healing of the need to sin, so that their lives can unfold as My honest, free, and loving children.

"This means that in one situation you may do something which seems ridiculously permissive in order to show love to someone who has sinned (as I did in the New Testament account of the woman taken in adultery) or to receive a repentant sinner back into My family (as I indicated in the parable of the Prodigal Son). In another situation, under seemingly similar circumstances, you may stand up and confront the sin and the sinner with the strong claims of justice—as I did with the Pharisees and in the temple. And the agony of the decision whether to emphasize love or justice— both are always involved for My people—is *in your hands.* That's why you cannot treat all crimes and sins and failures alike. If you want to do it My way, you've got to try to find out what's going on inside the people."

"I think I see," I said. "And I suppose some of us might be like a third child who *avoids* stealing the cookie just in order to be 'one up' on her sisters and to impress her Daddy. When you understand why she *didn't* steal, you realize that she can't be considered much more righteous than her sisters."

He smiled and said, "Now you are beginning to see the problem Jesus had with the Pharisees and their 'righteousness,' and to understand why most people don't like the Prodigal Son's older brother. But Keith, don't misinterpret this. I am *not* saying that the law is unimportant. I'm just saying that you've got to *fulfill the law* by always carrying love as well as justice with you into each situation. And I'm hoping that you will always try to see the one who commits the crime or the sin or experiences the failure through the lens of love."

I had been listening very carefully to most of the Presence's explanation, but now I began to squirm. Finally I said hesitantly, "Listen, Lord, I hate to interrupt this conversation, but I . . . I've got a problem."

"And what's that?"

"I . . . ah . . . I have to go to the bathroom."

"Oh, all right, we'll stop by your house." And suddenly, I was in my bed waking up. So I got up, went to the bathroom, came back and went to sleep.

8

"Keith. Keith? KEITH! It's time to go. We've got a lot of things to see and not much time in which to see them."

As I clung to Him we shot right through the wall, and again I marveled that we didn't touch a thing. It occurred to me that this must be how the disciples had felt when Jesus walked into that locked room after the crucifixion the first Easter evening. As we flew at that silent, almost blinding speed, I realized that there was something I'd been wanting to ask all my life. I was really afraid to ask it, but it occurred to me that this might be my only chance. I cleared my throat.

"Sir," I said carefully, "I've got something that I've wanted to ask You for years, but that I'm really afraid to ask, because whatever Your answer is I know some people who will be angry at me for bringing it up. What I want to ask You about concerns our interpretation of the Bible. But if the answer You give me is not what some people think it should be, I'm going to get murdered."

The Presence smiled tolerantly and said, "You sure are dramatic! Why would they bother you for telling them truth that is going to make them free? I told them years ago in the New Testament that the truth would make them free."

"Yes, Sir, I remember, but as I recall, *You* didn't do too well when You told them *personally*. Look what they did to You."

"Yes, well, what's your question?"

"Are we really supposed to believe the Scriptures literally? The academic theologians are brilliant, but as You know they disagree hotly about this. How are we supposed to view the Bible?"

"Hmmm," He said, looking below. "Let's find a place to sit down and talk about that." We circled toward a cliff jutting out from the largest mountain in the area. As we settled down with our feet dangling over the ledge, we could look far out over a mountain range and see the moonlight adding silver glitter to the snow-capped peaks in the distance.

"Keith, I really don't know how to tell you this, because it's going to come as such a big surprise to a lot of people. But I've never really been very interested in academic theology. I'm primarily interested in love—My love for people, their love for Me and for each other. And if the men and women who were arguing about these theological questions were loving each other, I wouldn't mind their arguing theology. But they aren't . . ."

He stopped and looked at me. "You looked surprised when I said I'm not all that interested in theology," He said, smiling. "But just think about it a minute. If My main interest had been in theology itself, why wouldn't I have given the church a book of clear theological propositions? I certainly have the mind for it! The trouble is, if I had done that, only those who are well educated in theology could understand the gospel! And I didn't want to play that kind of unfair 'mind game' with you, so I gave you a book of drama—narrative stories embedded in the history of a people. You have to find Me in the story of the Bible and trust Me on the basis of what you find—something that a child often has a chance of doing as well or even better than a theologian.

"And woven through the biblical accounts are some very *big* ideas that I wanted to get across. The main thing I tried to say in a hundred ways is that I really love *all of you;* and that, if you'll put your trust in Me, then there is no sin, no failure, no challenge too great for Me to handle and to help you handle . . . even death. When I hear people getting furious with each other in the body of believers over some contentious point about something like the virgin birth, I just have to shake My head and a deep sadness comes over Me."

"Well, what *about* the virgin birth?" I interrupted, afraid He was going on to something else. "For years one of my churchgoing friends has told me that he can believe in you as Creator, but he can't be a truly committed Christian because he can't believe in the virgin birth."

The Presence pursed His lips and looked at me thoughtfully. "It seems to me that your friend is gagging at gnats and swallowing camels," He said over a gentle chuckle. "In the first place, if he believes in an omnipotent God who could create the whole world out of nothing, then a little miracle like the virgin birth is nothing by comparison. And in the second place, if Jesus is who He said He was, then my sending Him by way of conception—however unusual—was the *least* miraculous way to go. Think about it. If I am who I am, then I could have sent Him in a sealed tin can! Now, *that* would have been a real miracle.

"But I know this is a serious problem for some people. So you might suggest to your friend that he commit as much of himself as he can to as much of Me as he can understand. Tell him that within that committed relationship I can teach him a true way of seeing that will free him to live creatively with questions like the technical aspects of Mary's virginity.

"Just remember, Keith, in the Bible I hardly ever gave the kinds of 'yes or no' theological answers you ask of each other. I almost always gave you a story or a parable. And *through* that story you could find the central truth I was trying to express—the truth about Me and about how I was reconciling the world to Myself.

"You theological types," He continued, "are always trying to pin Me down to *your* kind of logic, to *your* way of controlling truth, just like Nicodemus and the Pharisees did. But remember how many times in the Bible I refused to reveal Myself except through a story? And I have always done it as simply and as naturally as I could. If you've really studied the New Testament, you already know that I didn't succumb to the temptation to 'prove' the truth of My message through outlandish showy displays of power. I deliberately refrained from giving you 'answers' to questions you need to live through, because it is in living through the big questions of life that you can grow into the loving, trusting people I made you to be.

"Keith, I've got to say it once more: I never intended the New Testament to be a rule book or a book of scientific explanations. From the beginning, I meant it to be a means through which My people could get to know Me personally, to know My will, and to share in the salvation and life I have offered to all people. It makes My heart ache to see My children arguing and fighting and separating themselves over some of the details on which you people get hung up."

I was struggling not to get confused again, "Wait," I said, very concerned, "are you saying the theology isn't important, that it *doesn't matter* what we believe?"

The Presence just shook His head as if He couldn't imagine what He was hearing. And then He said as patiently as possible, "Of course I'm not saying that, Keith. People who say they just 'love God and aren't interested in theology,' have got to realize that without any 'theology' they don't have any way of knowing what *kind* of God it is they love. In other words, is the God they believe in a God who hates people? One who loves them? One who is vindictive and wants to stamp them out when they displease Him? Or is their God one who is just and yet forgives them and gives them new beginnings? Is their God capricious, or is He a God of order? Just what *kind* of a God are you dealing with? Your *theology* consists of what you use to answer these and other very important questions. So theology *is* important. Sooner or later you *must* think about your faith if you are a responsible Christian. It's crucial.

"But there is another paradox here: Although it is important to know what you believe, it is infinitely *more* important to love Me and other people and to *live* your belief in response to what you do know about Me. If you don't do this, it really doesn't matter much to Me what you believe about Christianity, because I'll know that you have missed the point of the whole Bible. As a matter of fact, thinking and arguing about theology is so far in third place—behind loving people and living your faith—that I can hardly see it by comparison."

He stopped, raised His eyebrows and shook His head as He had done so often all evening. Then He went on, "I look around in My church and see sophisticated teachers whose theology is far more in order than their lives are. And I see other people whose theology is lousy, but who are much closer to Me and to My kingdom than some of the leaders in the church. I tried to make that clear in the twenty-fifth chapter of Matthew when I told you the story of the judgment. There are going to be some real surprises at the end when people see how I feel about the essential nature of loving.

"The paradox about interpreting the Bible is that on one hand I want you to take the Bible very, very seriously. I want you to read it prayerfully *as My truth that I have revealed* in the lives of the Hebrew people for your salvation and sustenance. And I want you to know that all that is necessary for your salvation is found in the Scriptures. But on the other hand, even though I want you to take the Scriptures into your life both through your mind and heart, I do *not* want you to get hung up on the literal meaning of each word.

"I have seldom revealed myself with the logical precision your theologians sometimes seem to imply. And if you start arguing about those questions, a great wrong begins to take place: bitterness and antagonism replace love. It's not so much the 'facts' at issue that you are wrong about—one way or the other. But your *attitude* is wrong when you try to control and defeat other Christians as if they were opponents or even enemies.

"So I am hoping that the theologians among My people will begin to meet in a humble attitude of love and prayer—since *none* of them really understands all that much about Me and My will. My prayer is that someday people may say about My theologians, 'See how they love one another'—something I do not recall anyone's having said yet.

"The Scripture is both a sword and a shield, Keith. It will help you carve out a life in this world as I meant it to be lived, and it will defend you against evil. You don't have to defend it or justify your belief in what it says. In any case, only your *behavior* will reveal what you *really believe* about My Word. And you certainly don't have to defend *Me.* I appreciate the thought, but I simply don't need it. I'll be here after *all of you* are gone—and so will My Word!"

I just looked at Him. I really didn't know what to say. I wasn't sure I understood all that He meant, but I knew in my bones that it was awfully important. Finally, He said, "Come on, let's go. This kind of discussion hardly ever gets anywhere. We've got to get a move on."

9

The Presence glanced at my watch and said, "There isn't much time. We're going to go to two meetings in churches right across the street from each other. They're both having strategy meetings of their evangelism committees—only the first church calls evangelism 'church growth' because so many people are turned off by the word *evangelism*."

We breezed in and sat down in the corner of a large room which had been set up with chairs for about a hundred people. There were about fifteen or twenty mustered near the front, and the meeting was already going on. The woman who was speaking was about fifty years old and pleasingly plump, upholstered in a very fine tweed suit made of Scottish wool. She was obviously an important person on the committee and was giving her views regarding what evangelism meant to her: ". . . In conclusion, I'd just like to say that for me evangelism has always been a matter of *living* my faith. I don't have to *talk* about it if I am a sensitive, loving person."

She smiled with just the right amount of hesitant

warmth to be in good taste, and there was a polite smattering of applause as she settled onto a chair in the front row. As the applause stopped, a man who was obviously the leader of the meeting stood and said, smiling, "Thank you, Mrs. Burtrum." He then turned to the group and continued in a different and more businesslike tone, "Does anyone else have anything you'd like to say about evangelism or church growth before we begin talking about possible programs for this year?"

There were a few seconds of embarrassed silence, and finally a small, frail-looking woman sitting to one side of the group raised her hand. "Mary," the frail-looking woman said to the lady in the tweed suit, "As you know, this is my first meeting in this church, and I probably shouldn't speak at all. But I . . . well . . . I don't know how to say this, but recently I was in the hospital for a month following major surgery. And while I was there I got to know one of the nurses pretty well. She was such a radiant person I finally asked her, 'what *is* it that makes you so happy?' When she saw that I was serious, she told me about her relationship with Jesus Christ and what it had meant to her. She told me how He had changed her life and her relationships. She was so happy that she wanted to show love to everybody around her and to tell them that God could change their lives, too."

The frail woman looked out the window for a second, blinking back a tear, and then looked at the group and said, "I asked her how I could become a Christian. And she explained to me very simply how I could begin right then by surrendering as much of my life as I could to Jesus Christ. She said that the Holy Spirit and God's people in the Church would teach me how to become

76

a free, whole person. She said I'd learn how to witness to Him and help other people discover how they can find Him and His Way.

"So I made a beginning commitment of my life to Christ right there in that hospital bed. And, for the first time since I can remember, I began to feel a sense of peace about living. When I got home, I came down and joined this church."

The frail woman paused and looked down at her fingers, which were intertwined in her lap. Finally she continued. "Mary, I don't want to be critical of what you just said about a Christian not having to talk about her faith to evangelize people, but I've been playing bridge with you and our friends in this church for twenty years. I was crying out for a faith to live by, and none of you ever even told me that you were Christians! You never said anything about Jesus Christ or about how your lives had changed because of Him. I almost went down the drain starving for God—and here I was surrounded by Christian leaders all those years, without even knowing it."

I turned to the Presence and gave a low whistle. He nodded his head and waved His hand toward the window, letting me know we were going to the other meeting.

The second gathering was also an evangelism planning meeting, but this one was filled with people. There must have been a hundred fifty people in a room with about a hundred seventy chairs. We sat in two of the empty seats in the back and watched what appeared to be a heated argument between two men standing at different places in the crowd.

The first man, who was about forty, was dressed in

a light blue suit with a swirling blue-and-white tie. He was saying with a very rapid-fire delivery, "With this new system, we can divide the city up into sections, and if every person commits to knock on twenty doors within the next two months, we will have converted a substantial part of the whole city—especially if we start in the influential neighborhoods."

The other man, who had evidently just stood up while the first was talking, interrupted him. "Wait a minute, wait a minute, John. You act as if we're 'selling tickets to heaven.' It seems to me that these are *people* we're calling on. We need to spend some time listening to them, finding out who they are and what they see their needs to be, before we jump down their throats with three scriptures and a poem and try to talk them into the kingdom. We're not just asking them for a verbal commitment to Jesus; we're asking them to *turn their whole lives over to Almighty God from now on—forever!* This kind of commitment is more serious than marriage— the deepest commitment in human life—and you're making it like we're recruiting people for our bowling team. I'd be embarrassed to go out that way."

The other man's face and neck were getting red with anger as he said, "What's the matter, Jim; are you afraid of witnessing? I'm committed to witnessing to every person I see and to telling them the claims of Christ on their life."

"Even before they know you—or know about your faith—or have *any* reason to trust you?" Jim asked angrily.

Just then the man leading the meeting said, "What we've got to do is get back to the Bible. We need to quote the scriptures to them—get them into the Word."

"Not until you at least find out who they are!" Jim said.

I started to say something when the Presence squeezed my arm hard and whispered, "Let's get out of here. I already know how this argument's going to turn out." And we could hear the people almost shouting at each other about how to "love the world" as we sailed out of the window.

10

In a few minutes, as we were flying high above the trees, another question occurred to me. The Presence was very silent and grim looking. "Excuse me," I said, "If this is not a good time to ask, let me know, but something is really bothering me."

"That's all right, go ahead."

"Well, those people back there had such different ideas about what evangelism was that you'd hardly know they were talking about the same thing. What did *you* mean when you invented the idea of evangelism?"

"Well, you'd never believe it, Keith, but the reason I chose that word was that it simply means 'to announce good news.' "

"I think I know, but what exactly *is* the Good News?" The Presence gazed off in the distance for a minute, and then He said, "You contemporary Christians have made it so complicated that sometimes even I have trouble remembering exactly what it is. The original Good News which the New Testament announced was that at last there had broken into the world a New Way—My way—

of living and doing things in love. I called this way of living My reign, or kingdom. Through Jesus I was announcing that My kingdom had come, and that I was prepared to forgive all people and give them new life. And My love and the power to bring this kingdom into actuality was demonstrated and made concrete through the life, death, and resurrection of Jesus.

"After Jesus left, My Spirit, My Personality, which the disciples had experienced in Jesus, was released to be *in* My people—to free them to love each other and the world. Through My Spirit you all are going to know personally and intimately that I love you, and that you are secure in that love forever, even beyond death. And because you have that security, you don't have to hurt each other and compete for all the good things in life. Instead, you can share and enjoy living and working, loving, and dancing together—as David danced before the ark. That's why the whole message is called *Good News*."

"Why don't we see people in the church living and loving and dancing together since Jesus announced the coming of the Kingdom?"

The Presence looked thoughtful. "That's a good question."

"Well, I've got another one for You. Remember those people back there arguing about how to do evangelism— some wanting to go out and preach and say Bible verses when they knock on people's doors, and others saying it was a better idea to start by listening to people and finding out where they hurt and *then* witnessing to them? Which way is *Your* way?"

The Presence looked at me with that same sad look I had seen before. He said, "Keith, why do you always

81

keep asking questions like that? Sounds to me like you are trying to get me to justify *your* way. I have given different people different gifts, and there isn't just one gift—or one way to *exercise* a gift—in a church. Not everybody is supposed to preach and quote Bible verses. Some people are called simply to tell other people what's happened in their lives because of making a commitment to Jesus Christ—like the nurse told the woman in the hospital. People who do this are called 'witnesses.' And a witness (as in a court case) is not supposed to do anything except describe first-hand what she or he has seen and heard. In other words, witnesses are not necessarily called to be theologians. But most programs on evangelism try to make theologians out of lay witnesses and teach them how to *explain* the theology of the Incarnation. And many of them do a terrible job.

"Besides, most people are brought into the kingdom because somebody—like the nurse in the hospital—took the time to love them and pay special attention to them, not because they grasped a great understanding of the content of the gospel message itself. And without that loving being involved at some level, the *essence* of the gospel is never transmitted in any case."

"I thought You said evangelism was announcing the Good News."

"Well, yes," He said, "but there are two aspects to the Good News, and they are intertwined. There is the Good News announced by Jesus in the New Testament that My kingdom is coming, and then there's the Good News of what happened to you personally because of having committed your life to Christ. The people who are given the 'gift' of evangelism are those who announce the part about the kingdom and the Cross. Everybody else is at least a witness (though some witnesses may be also called to do things like teach or prophesy).

"As far as using the Scripture is concerned," He went on, "in the New Testament I used it mostly when talking to Satan. I did use it to teach the disciples how to interpret what the coming of the kingdom meant. But when talking to the people outside the disciple-group, I almost always told stories and spoke in parables. I have found that most people, especially people outside the church, simply don't assimilate theological ideas in a way that reaches deep inside them, where they really live. Maybe they can sometimes, but only very rarely. On the other hand, almost anybody can respond to a witness's account of how his or her life has been changed by making a commitment to Me.

"Besides, since the Crucifixion and Resurrection happened two thousand years ago, those events seem like past history to most people outside the faith. But what happened to a lay person in his or her life *this morning* (or last week) is a little harder to deny as an experience to be taken seriously."

"Oh," I said thoughtfully, "I think I see. But there's one thing about the way You've been talking all night that confuses me. Sometimes You speak of Jesus as 'I' and sometimes as 'He.' Why is that?"

The Presence smiled and said with a twinkle in His eye, "Well, Keith, that's just one of the complications of living in the Trinity."

Suddenly He looked down at the rolling blackness below, quilted with a thousand pinpoints of light. He took a deep breath and said, "Watch it, here we go again."

As the wind whistled in my ears the Presence commented (loudly, so I could hear), "In one way she was right, you know—that first lady in the tweed suit—when she said that a lot of evangelism is done simply by being a loving person. If you aren't a genuinely loving person, not many people will care about what you believe concerning Me."

"Hmmm," I said and changed the subject, "Why were You so upset when I almost spoke out in that meeting?"

"Well, it wasn't so much that I was mad at you. I was mostly just frustrated at what was going on. I saw again that some of you contemporary Christians are ashamed even to mention My name, and others of you (who are talking about Me all of the time) don't seem to care about the feelings and experienced needs of the people you are evangelizing. And by being insensitive and treating the gospel like a quick ticket to safety, you trivialize the greatest message I ever gave to the world. You treat it like some kind of word game in which people are supposed to 'say the right thing' and then their lives will be changed. Keith, the whole name of the game of evangelism is loving people for My sake—which My Spirit may use to lead people to *conversion!*"

"Well," I said laughing, "If You think the word *evangelism* turns people off, You should try using the word *conversion* around our church. By the way, what's the difference between conversion and joining the church? And how does conversion happen, anyway?"

"All right," He said, "and I know that people really get bent out of shape about whether someone has 'been converted' or not, according to their own formula—as if I would only love people who had said a certain set of words some evangelist made up. But Keith, as I've told you all evening, I love *all* My children—inside and outside the church. As Paul explained, I loved you just as surely *before* you became Christians as after. But I've made you in such a way that only as you accept My love can you become whole and fulfilled and be with Me forever. So conversion isn't something you do to get in better with Me; it's a way for you to choose to channel your faith in My life and work (and that, of course, will make us both very happy).

"But sometimes the act of joining a Church can be like getting initiated into a civic club. They ask a person some questions about the faith and he or she answers them. And if the person answers the right way, they take him or her down to the front of the church and make him/her a member. Unfortunately, it's very common for someone to answer all the questions correctly and be fully accepted into a church and still not really be converted.

"Authentic conversion," He continued, "happens in many different ways, but basically it happens when people find out they really can't live without Me. Then (usually through the love of one of you Christians), they begin to feel enough love and trust in Me that they come to a point at which they can turn from their frustrating, self-centered lives with a strong desire to change. Then at some point they decide—or discover they have already decided—to *commit their whole lives to Me* as they see Me in Jesus. Some people come to this point through personal tragedies and dramatic circumstances, and others arrive quietly through an internal awareness of who I am and who they are. But in either case, through conversion I can give them a creative new agenda for their lives. And then they begin to experience the joy and hope and wonder they were meant to have—because they are made to be like Me, and I'm the source and epitome of all of these things."

11

"We're coming to our last stop," the Presence said. "Get ready!" I closed my eyes and huddled close as I started somersaulting in the air. When I opened my eyes the time had changed to two o'clock in the afternoon, and we were floating into the large third-floor meeting room of a denominational headquarters. A group of about forty-five ministers were evidently engaged in a planning meeting. Across the top of the blackboard was written, "New Life in the Church Conference." Below was a subheading: "Speakers and Leaders." And the names listed here all had the prefix, *Rev.*

A young black minister was standing, having been recognized by the chairman. The young man pointed to the blackboard and said, "Wait a minute, why don't we have any *lay* people on that list? They're the ones who gave us the mandate to put on this conference at the last general convention." There was an awkward silence as everyone looked at the blackboard.

A handsome man about forty-five years old, with blond hair and blue eyes, leaned back in his chair and spoke from where he was sitting. "John, we talked about this in the steering committee and decided that, since this conference may set the tone for the church during the coming decade, it's extremely important that the renewal of the church be outlined by responsible voices. And the laity simply don't have the theological education. As we all know, the theological implications of the Incarnation are incredibly complex. And to turn the next chapter of the church's history over to a bunch of theologically uneducated people seems insane."

He paused, and concluded, "John, we all had these idealistic thoughts about what the laity can do when we were first ordained. But, well, after a few years I think you'll realize that what I'm saying is true."

Silence. The chairman looked with raised eyebrows at the young minister who'd brought up the question, but who now sat down without responding. Then the chairman looked down at his notes and started to go on.

But suddenly the younger man was on his feet again. "Insane?—the idea of trusting a group of theologically uneducated people with the future of the church— insane? Then why did God *do that very thing when the church was born?* Good Lord, I just saw how blind we've become. Do you think there weren't any trained Jewish theologians and priests around in first century Palestine? There were probably more per capita back then than there are in the church today! But God bypassed them, and He gave the new church to the laity. If I had to guess why, I'd say it was probably because the 'preachers' then were so rigid and proud and protective—afraid that God might do something without them through the lives of the laity. And if He *did* do something significant without them, the preachers might *lose control* of God's people and be revealed as inadequate and fearful, as they secretly felt they were—just like us!!"

Silence. No one even glanced at the young man. He just stood there looking over the group, amazed that no one said anything.

Finally, the chairman spoke, "Well . . . uh . . . John, thank you for your input, but we've really got to move on . . ."

The young man sat down again, discouraged.

The chairman went on, "The second item on the agenda has to do with workshops. It is the steering committee's recommendation that the various racial groups in our constituency be represented and a strong woman or two be included. First the committee prepared a list of top . . ."

I felt a jerk of my upper arm and suddenly we were rising above the tree tops at what felt like a Mach IV speed. I noticed that there were tears on the Presence's cheeks as He said, "They have eyes, I gave them all eyes. But they can't see. That young black minister spoke the simple truth, and *he* wound up looking naïve in that meeting. But he was right: I did choose primarily lay people to build My church in the beginning. I chose them because they were grasped by the enormity of the gift of My love and forgiveness and of new life. They didn't try to reduce the gospel to a subject to be studied, like 'mathematics' or 'theology'; they saw it as a *way to live* together with Me as a personal Member of their company.

"I could trust those theologically uneducated lay people not to get too far from Me on the journey *because* they *listened to Me* before they decided who was to go where or do what. And they understood that I am *alive* and would be going on the journey with them in My Spirit to teach them and strengthen them! They were not limited and bound by the prison walls of logic, as you people who have been to graduate school so often are.

"Do those arrogant ministers back there think they are the only ones who can interpret what I am *saying today* to My people whose hearts are open to Me—just because those ministers read Greek? Keith, I am a *living Communicator,* not just an ancient historical figure on a mountain . . . or even on a cross! I am *alive,* as you are alive, but so many ministers' overt behavior indicates that at a practical level they simply do not believe that!"

He stopped speaking and shook His head sadly. "Besides," He continued offhandedly, "I didn't even speak Greek when I was living on earth; I spoke Aramaic. And I liked working with My hands. My favorite subject in school was 'shop.' I was very well-versed in Scripture, but I certainly wasn't a professional scholar."

I was confused again. "Don't You want us to apply our minds to learning all we can about You?" I asked hesitantly.

"Of course I do!" He almost shouted, "but don't you remember how many different times and ways Jesus tried to tell His followers that logic and foolishness are often married to each other, and that people could only see the things of the Kingdom through a 'birthing' transition from the intellect to the intuition? It was 'like being born again' Jesus said, and that's certainly an intuitive and not a logical truth. The naïveté of those ministers back there in that meeting, thinking that a person has to have a theological degree to lead renewal in the church, is so incredible that I wouldn't believe what I heard . . . except that I hear the same thing every day in so many churches I hang around.

"Keith, I didn't come in Jesus Christ to make people

89

brilliant theologians. I didn't come to give people a great treatise on 'sight'; I came to *heal their blindness* so they themselves can see and then help others to see. Theological education is a great help for teaching people who can already see, but it *does nothing to cure blindness!*

"A layperson saying simply and with obvious integrity, 'I was blind and now I can see!' may do more to start renewal in the church than nine sermons about the gospel tradition of healing in Mark. I *know* you need both, but I am sad and upset when I think that knowing *about* Me has been assigned more relative value than the continuing experience of *actually communicating with me!*"

He stopped a moment, His anger having subsided with the outburst.

I finally said hesitantly, "I'm not trying to contradict what You just said, but I've been working in the lay renewal movement for twenty-five years, and quite honestly I don't think most lay people would have the foggiest idea of how to run the institutional church if you gave it to them on a platter. I think the church would fall back a thousand years in the hands of the laity."

He smiled whimsically, "In some ways," He said, "I would hope *two* thousand—not literally of course; but in terms of the way *the church actually, personally relates to Me in its practical day-to-day living.* Keith, don't you see the spiritual monstrosities denominational officials have made out of many of their boards? The way many denominational bureaucracies work has almost nothing to do with the idea of living vulnerably as converted people, dependent hour by hour on the awareness of my Presence in a contemporary outpost of My kingdom? Many such church leaders are almost more reticent to pray together informally and vulnerably than a group of government officials might be."

"That can't be true!"

"But it *is* true, Keith. I can hardly remember the last time I heard a group of people in a denominational bureaucracy sitting down together to share their lives in confession and prayer and listening for My voice. Some of those people don't even *believe* in a personal relationship with Me any more and would secretly like to leave."

"Why do they stay then?"

"Because they do believe in the church, and in Me in a general sort of way, and because frankly some of them have worked for their denomination for years and don't have anywhere else to go."

"Wait a minute, Sir," I interrupted, a little hesitant to do so, "but You really seem to be jumping on the clergy, especially those in the higher levels of church structure. Are You saying it's all their fault that the church is in such bad shape?"

"No," He said evenly, "it's the fault of all of you— lay and clergy—who praise Me with your lips and secretly follow the gods of your own success or comfort or lust. The reason I'm jumping on the denominational leaders is that they have committed themselves to be the shepherds, the leaders, of My flock. I count on them to be the models of integrity and commitment and love for My people. And when their shepherds turn away from Me, the sheep lose direction and wander away from the flock."

"That's a terrible responsibility," I said.

"It really isn't an easy row to hoe," He admitted. "But Keith, there *are* some great and sensitive leaders in all the denominations. The trouble is that they are often labeled as idealists and shunted aside or 'listened to' and then 'worked around' when the practical decisions are made. It's very sad, and the average layperson paying the bills has no idea of the secular ambience of much high-level denominational thinking."

"But if we didn't have the denominational structures," I said, "the church would fall apart. Don't you believe in the unity of larger church?"

He frowned. "What 'unity' is that, Keith? Since the late Middle Ages the only real 'larger unity' My church has had is the mystical unity of all those committed to My Son. The present institutional 'unity of the larger church' which you speak of is a myth. But we were talking about denominational structures.

"And Keith, if *all* the denominational heirarchies in the world were destroyed tomorrow, there's a strong possibility that My church would be more *alive* and *real* in forty-eight hours than it has been in the last hundred years!"

"How??"

"Well, the committed Christians would get together locally in groups and *call on Me*. With My Spirit in them and *having to depend on Me and on each other,* they would pray and read My Word and be sustained by the body and blood of My Son in a way many of them haven't been in years. They'd have a greater tendency to love the people around them because they would know there wasn't any denominational bureau to do it for them. And wherever they went they would take with them the healing they'd be discovering in their life together.

"Oh, it would be scary and messy and chaotic—not nearly as orderly and neat as the keepers of the system have made it. And there would be some ghastly mistakes made. But in a way it would be *glorious!* It would be *real!* And My Presence would be experienced everywhere!"

He looked at me with His eyes shining. "Keith," He said, "I love the church with all My heart, and I want to keep it alive and close to Me! The denominational structures are often helpful tools for the propagation and continuance of the faith, but don't think for a minute that My Church would die in the hands of committed lay people. I intend for the clergy and denominational officials to be My player-coaches. But if they become afraid to be real and get possessive of My power and hide from Me in their personal lives, I'll throw them out of the Garden again. And I'll raise up a whole new group of leaders to breathe life back into the body of the church."

"I can't see You doing that. Those people have worked long and hard and given their lives for the church. It would be unthinkable—besides, no one would believe it was You who was doing it. And the hierarchy would be shocked out of their socks. I just don't think You'd do it."

"Oh, wouldn't I?" He said, "Well, that's exactly what I did in the Protestant Reformation—and you don't think the church's hierarchy was shocked then?"

I found myself smiling as I shook my head, imagining the effect of my telling the church what He'd just said. He saw me and said with cold steel in His voice, "Everything I've said about being replaceable in the church goes for *you, too,* Miller. Your complacency and failure to get involved continually amazes me, especially in light of all I've done for you."

As He said those words I felt ashamed of the way I have been critical of the church's hierarchy, but not willing to pay the price of getting in the institutional flow enough to try to change things. But I also knew that any kind of significant change in an institution is really hard to come by, and I felt that the Presence was not being realistic. I asked Him, "Don't You think You are being idealistic and unreal in suggesting that the men in that renewal planning meeting back there try to deal with the black minister's scathing critique? I never know what to say in a meeting when someone makes an impassioned statement the way he did."

The Presence looked a million years old as He said, "Yes, Keith, I *know* how hard it is even to *hear* the truth that one needs to change, much less acknowledge it and deal with it. But the committee buried that young man's clear strong voice by acting as if he had never spoken, and that hurts. In a world with freedom of choice there must be prophets to call you back to the truth—even if they sound rash, unrealistic, and terribly impractical. Otherwise, how can you ever get back on track and grow into what I made you to be?"

"But," I said, wagging my head, "if I'd been rejected at close range by my peers the way that young man was, I wouldn't even *want* to come to another meeting of that group. They treated him like an ignorant kid. What happens to those who keep coming back to the meetings and saying the truth—even in the face of censure and rejection?"

The Presence smiled with a faraway look in His eye, as if He were seeing in His memory people He knew. "Well," He said, laughing gently, "for one thing they often grow very close to Me." Then He looked serious as He continued, "and in the end many of them are really lonely. Some are destroyed vocationally or even killed. But—even though they sometimes don't live to see the fruits of their work—it's often through their efforts that My people come back to Me."

"That's sure a strange way to do it," I said thoughtfully.

"Yes, it is," He answered, "but since I've given you free will, it's about the only way I can get your attention enough to get the job done with integrity. Unfortunately, there is almost always a lot of pain in the really serious kind of loving that I'm calling you Christians to do. I ask people to risk rejection by saying the truth in love, knowing it will take a miracle for someone really to hear and then have the courage to stand up and blow the whistle on the shoddy and dishonest manipulations into which My people keep falling."

I was feeling a little overwhelmed with all that I'd heard and seen, and I certainly didn't see myself as anybody who wanted to tell the church all that. Why me? Suddenly I felt depressed and a little irritated with the Presence. And I said, "It seems to me that You are attacking the church at a time when she's so weak she doesn't have a chance of being strong. It doesn't take a lot of courage to do that . . . Sir."

He looked at me, knowing the irritation in my voice came from my fear of rejection and failure, and replied, "Ah, you are so wrong, Keith, about the church's not having a chance of being strong. When she seems weakest and most desperate, she is actually *closest* to being her strongest—because she is closest to *giving up* trying to 'do it in her *own* strength.' And when she has almost reached the end of her rope, she is nearest to *seeing her sin, repenting, and turning her life back over to Me!* When those things happen, the church can be renewed.

"But until the church leaders see the incredible distance

with which they have separated themselves and their operations from a personal commitment to Me and to finding and doing My will, until they see somehow and repent, authentic renewal of the existing churches just isn't going to happen—even with the best new programs in the world. The church is weak only when she loses her integrity and her primary commitment to Me, and that's why I want you to tell My people what I've shown you.

"When she is faithful and honest, the church is an invincible moral force that can crumple empires! And the strange thing is that her real strength has never been in numbers of members but in the passionate commitment of those few who have 'heard' and decided to put their whole lives into being My followers. So if My people see their sin and repent and come back to Me today, then in that *very hour* the church will *immediately* be the strongest moral and spiritual force in the world!

"Look," He interrupted Himself, pointing ahead, "You're almost home."

12

As I looked down, I began to see familiar sights. We'd just passed over Victoria, Texas, far below, and were sailing along above Highway 77 toward home. I could see the lights of Rockport ahead to the left and realized that we'd soon be back in Port Aransas.

"How do you feel?" the Presence asked.

"Well, I'm scared. If I tell the people the truth You showed me tonight, I don't know what will happen to me. I don't think the church can really hear that in many ways You think it is being selfish, materialistic, cowardly, and incredibly self-deceptive. Its sermons and liturgy say one thing, but much of its everyday life and many of its programs say something different. It's as if people believe the sermons and liturgy are about something that was real two thousand years ago, but not today—as if You aren't really alive anymore.

"People will probably be horrified if they actually grasp the fact that the issues on which they spend so much of their creative time—issues like building funds, budgets, church bazaars, teas, circle meetings, and luncheons—are hardly interesting to You at all. According to what I've seen with You tonight, You have a whole different set of priorities—integrity, conversion, sacrificial loving, feeding the poor, and using *most* of the church's budget to help people beyond the congregation. You *really want* us to be peacemakers and to make sure that every group and person is loved, accepted, and offered a real place in the heart of Your family. Yet, I hear You saying that churches which spend most of their creative time on these issues are very rare.

"Lord," I continued, "I know a little about people, and I know myself, and we don't like hearing about our own greatest problems—especially those we've avoided facing. And if I tell people what You've shown me tonight, they may ostracize me. Can You see me getting on a Christian radio or TV program after this?"

The Presence didn't say anything, but looked ahead. We had come to the coast, turned south, and were starting to wing toward home as I repeated, "Really, Lord, I'm uneasy. Doing this may ruin me vocationally!"

The Presence turned and, for a long moment, looked deep inside me with compassion and love. Then He nodded His head. "Yes," He said, "I know."

I had been about to panic. But now, as I thought about what it had meant just to be with Him those few hours, I felt strangely at peace. If He loved me—and that look had said it all—then why did I have to fear a bunch of people who didn't really understand me anyway? I didn't! (But even as I said that to myself, a little voice inside me added, "At least for now.")

We had settled on top of a large palm tree in our front yard and were watching as the moonlight made a silver-orange highway across the rolling surf. In my mind's eye I saw a kaleidoscope of pictures of all the places we had been that night.

"All right," I said quietly, "I guess I'm going to tell them what I've seen. But," I blurted out, "what can You *do* about the mess Your church is in? Didn't You *plan* for this?" I didn't know what else to say. And didn't know if I even wanted Him to answer, because I was afraid there wouldn't be any answer.

But after a few seconds He said thoughtfully, "Keith, when I made each of you, I put inside you a kind of hope and renewing courage and a sort of 'unreality detector.' And these things will only let you go so far away from Me before you stop in disgust and consider turning away from your sin, self-centeredness, and greed—and coming back to Me. When you do turn, I'll always be there waiting for you.

"What I'm hoping is that My people will hear what you tell them, and know in their hearts that it's true. I'm dreaming that hundreds of them will turn again, offer their futures to Me and meet together in small clusters to pray and to learn to love each other and the hurting people in the world. And I hope some of them will stand up in church meetings all over the country and stop this dishonest charade and 'playing church' which is being done in the name of the gospel of Jesus Christ. The church is not supposed to be a club, with petty power struggles over money, bazaars, and teas, Keith, although you— My people—have made it into that.

"From the beginning, I have dreamed that My church will be *an outpost for the healing and transforming of the whole world*—an outpost of My love and courage! If some of My people hear these words, a flame can start; and if it does, it will grow. With My help, it can sweep through the Church today, as it has time after time in the past. And as this flame of My Spirit touches people, it will bring new life, integrity, meaning, hope, and My love to a world starving for those things.

"And if people only hear you and know that they are not crazy for being dismayed when they see the lack of reality and love around them in the church, it will all be worthwhile. But if you will speak, in love, the truth that I've shown you, I believe there may be men and women—young and old, within and outside the Church—who will see, repent, be converted, and go about really loving one another and the world in My name! That," He said with a tear of hope in His eye, "is My dream!"

I nodded my head, deeply touched by the love and compassion in His voice. "But," I said softly, "aren't You going to tell them how to do it?"

He smiled again with a twinkle in His eye. "One dream at a time, Keith. After all, you haven't decided for sure if you are going to tell them about this one yet. Besides," He added thoughtfully, "if anyone 'hears you' and is interested in living out My dream, if they'll come to Me, I'll guide them—each according to the particular gifts and circumstances I've given them."

As He was speaking these last words, He was laying me down in my bed. On my cheeks I felt hot tears of hope and happiness as I turned to tell Him how grateful I was for our time together. But He was gone.

When I opened my eyes, I was in my bed, waking up. I raised myself to my elbows and realized I had been asleep all night. It was almost dawn. I could hear the surf's steady throbbing against the shore outside. The pink-grey light of the coming day was filtering into the bedroom as I realized with an enormous wave of relief: *It was only a dream! And I didn't have to say anything to anyone about it!* I lay back in the bed and began to laugh.

But just at that moment, when I was totally awake, *I heard the voice again!* I couldn't tell if it was coming from somewhere above, outside, inside, or around me—I wasn't sure *where* it was coming from—but it was definitely His voice. And He was calling my name.

Now I was really terrified! The voice spoke again, as if from a great distance.

"Keith! Keith!"

"Yes?"

"Keith . . . don't forget to tell them that I love them!"

THE END.

PUBLISHER'S NOTE

If you have been touched by this story, Keith Miller has written a book which may interest you. That book is about living and sharing life as a Christian in a church setting, and in it the author suggests ways some of the problems set out in *The Dream* might be avoided. The title is *The Scent of Love*.